The Asquinn Twins
Book Five

Guardians Of Forest Lake

Grace Brooks

PUBLISHED by PARABLES
Earthly Stories with a Heavenly Meaning

The Asquinn Twins Book 5: Guardians of Forest Lake
Revised edition

Original Copyright 1987, updated 2004, 2009 and 2015

Copyright © Grace Brooks
December, 2016

Published By Parables
December, 2016

All Rights Reserved. No part of this book may be reproduced or utilized in any form or by any means, electronic or mechanical, including photocopying, recording, or by any information storage and retrieval system, without permission in writing from the author.

Unless otherwise specified Scripture quotations are taken from the authorized version of the King James Bible.

First Edition   March, 2006
Revised Edition October, 2016

ISBN 978-1-945698-19-4

Printed in the United States of America

Readers should be aware that Internet Web sites offered as citations and/or sources for further information may have been changed or disappeared between the time this was written and when it is read.

The Asquinn Twins
Book Five
Guardians Of Forest Lake

Grace Brooks

PUBLISHED by PARABLES
Earthly Stories with a Heavenly Meaning

Dedication

I dedicate this entire series to the Ontario Provincial Police

Chapter One

It was a hot day at the start of summer. Olvina Asquinn and her four sisters, along with her cousin Trevor Olverton, stood in a row in front of Ontario Provincial Police Chief Inspector Bradan Turehue.

Watching the proceedings in chairs close to where the teens stood were the twins: Martin, the girls' adoptive father, and Martha Turehue, the chief inspector's wife. Martin's wife, Audrey, sat beside him.

Bradan was the girls' and Trevor's uncle and second-in-command of the Forest Lake detachment.

Bradan was forty-two years old. Grey hairs sprinkled his short-cut hair.

Beside Bradan stood Chief Superintendent Kenneth Asquinn. He was in command of the Forest Lake Police Department. He was another of the girls' and Trevor's uncles. Today, Ken overlooked the procedures. He was also in his early forties, with salt-and-pepper hair

Each teen held up a right hand with the other on a Bible.

Once finished repeating their duty of oath, the teens lowered their hands. Bradan beamed at them.

Martin and Martha started clapping. Wapinkino, a youth with a Native background, and the girls' and Trevor's best friend, clapped his hands. He wasn't in the lineup as he didn't believe being a police cadet was for him. Not that he held any grudge against the police. Sihon, the quintuplet's adoptive brother, sat as a spectator beside him.

Olvina, Phoebe, Cassia, Kathleen, and Eunice were fraternal quintuplets, adopted by Martin and Audrey Asquinn when the girls were newborn babies. Three of the girls had light brown, sandy-colored hair while one had a reddish tinge with brown eyes; the middle girl's hair was black, her eyes blue. Sihon had been rescued from abusive parents and relatives that practiced witchcraft, being fostered before adopted.

There was another girl, younger than the five sisters and Sihon. Sihon and Crystal were first cousins, but she, too, had been pulled out of an abusive situation with her parents, Conrad and Lillian Cameron, who were Sihon's aunt and uncle. Martin and Audrey had gained custody of her. Now she was an adopted member of the family.

"Now, Olvina, Phoebe, Cassia, Kathleen, and Eunice Asquinn and Trevor Olverton, you are sworn in as Ontario Provincial Police cadets and are eager to assist me when Uncle Ken goes on vacation, right?"

"Right, Uncle Bradan," six voices said in unison.

"Dismissed," Bradan said.

Everyone stood and mingled. Olvina led the way to her parents. Martin and Audrey hugged Olvina and her sisters in one big hug.

"Congratulations," Martha smiled at the six.

Olvina turned to her blue-eyed uncle.

"Uncle Ken, you aren't going on vacation until after Morley's and Gay-Anne's wedding, right?"

Gay-Anne Asquinn was the girls', Sihon's, and Trevor's cousin.

"When are you leaving?" Martin asked.

"We will leave as soon as Morley and his bride return from their honeymoon," Ken replied.

***

One cool summer's evening, Olvina pushed the old man in the wheelchair up the access ramp to his new apartment. An old battered and dusty truck stood parked on one side of the driveway. The vehicle was almost as old as the old man. Cassia, Phoebe, Kathleen, and Eunice stood by the door.

"Mr. Greene," Cassia said, "welcome to your new home."

"I'm sure you will be more comfortable here than all by yourself way out on the outskirts of town," Eunice said.

The eighty-three-year-old man grunted. "I'll get used to living in an apartment in Forest Lake."

The group helped Mr. Greene inside and before leaving him, made sure he was comfortable.

"Dad will be around to give you a ride to church on Sunday," Olvina said as she closed the door behind her.

***

On the morning of their cousin's wedding, Olvina and her sisters stood at the back of the church. The five were Gay-Anne's flower girls. They wore ankle-length purple dresses with a matching shawl around their shoulders, and purple sandals.

The church full of guests listened to Ken and Bradan sing the wedding song.

On the organ, Esther Jamison, married to Owen Winschell Senior, began the notes of the wedding march. The wedding precession, led by Olvina, started down the center aisle, with Gay-Anne on her father's-- Eric Asquinn's, arm.

Olvina carried a basket of dark purple roses, while her sisters behind her carried matching bouquets. Eunice walked behind Gay-Anne and their uncle Eric, making sure the long white train of the bride's dress didn't get caught on anything.

Gay-Anne smiled broadly behind the veil over her face. She wore a floor-length white wedding dress, complete with a long-trailing train at the back.

The guests stood as the procession moved slowly by.

The pair to be married stood in front of Pastor Asquinn, the quintuplet's grandfather, which in Welsh was called "Tadcu."

Eric turned his daughter over to Morley then joined his family, which now consisted of only his wife June, and seventeen-year-old Danial.

Morley, dressed in black shoes, pants, jacket and white shirt and tie, smiled happily down at his bride-to-be. Gay-Anne smiled back at him.

"Dearly beloved," Pastor Asquinn began, "we are gathered together this day to join this man, Morley Todd Barclay, and this woman, Gay-Anne Asquinn, in holy matrimony."

The best man, Sihon Nigel Weistien-Asquinn, handed Morley the ring.

Morley reached for Gay-Anne's hand and slipped the ring on her finger.

"With this ring I do wed you, Gay-Anne Asquinn. This ring is a symbol of the circle of life. My love for you has no beginning or ending. It is eternal."

Olvina handed Gay-Anne the wedding ring. Gay-Anne slipped it onto Morley's finger.

"This ring also represents my love for you. Where the circle joins is a token of our lives and our love for one another, and like the circle, will never come apart. My love for you will never depart."

"I now pronounce you man and wife," Pastor Asquinn said then looked at Morley. "You may kiss the bride."

Morley drew back the veil and kissed her on the lips. He put an arm around her waist and Gay-Anne put an arm around his. Together they started the procession down the aisle.

Martin stood from where he watched with his family. "We will now gather out at Wischell's acreage for the reception. For those that don't know where to go, just follow the procession."

Martha and a few guests threw rice and confetti. The couple's real glory waited for them outside.

At the bottom of the church steps, an archway of policemen waited. Ken and Bradan stood closest to the last step and it was these two the newlyweds saw when they came outside.

His arm still around her waist, Morley led Gay-Anne to where a team of Percheron horses were hitched to a hansom buggy.

Olvina admired the horses as they stood proud and patient, their deep brown coats, light colored manes and tails gleaming in the sunlight. The polished harness rigging also shone in the sun.

Ken and Bradan hurried from the head of the arch to where Eric helped Gay-Anne into the buggy and seated her comfortably on the front seat.

As an honor guard, Bradan rode at the back on a little platform with only enough room for one. Olvina and her sisters rode in the back seat.

"Doesn't this make you sad to think about the police wedding we forfeited when we married before going west?" Aunt Charlotte, Ken's wife and Bradan's sister, asked.

"It certainly does," Martha, Bradan's wife and Ken's sister, agreed.

Ken hurried to the cruiser. He quickly got into position in front of the horses and started moving forward.

"Get up," fifteen-year-old Owen Jr. said. He clucked at the horses to get them moving.

The gravel road rounded a curve by a ridge. A house and open acres of land came into view. Mr. Greene's house, the one house he'd lived in for the girls didn't know how long. Now it was up for sale. But as the buggy plodded by, Olvina noticed a sold sign covered the for sale one. Olvina's heart leaped. It appeared Morley had bought the place for him and his new bride.

***

The following day, Monday, Olvina, dressed in blue culottes that resembled a split skirt. She also wore a light blue blouse. Olvina and her sisters liked wearing culottes because they looked like a split skirt. The box pleat split cutlottes functioned like long shorts but looked like a skirt. Olvina and her sisters wore cullottes as an alternative to pants.

Olvina made her way across vanLadislaves's Restaurant and Lake Tours parking lot. The business was owned by George vanLadislave. The parking lot was packed with vehicles. She walked backwards, facing the rest.

"How many of you remember Conrad Cameron?" Olvina said.

Trevor answered, "I sure do."

Phoebe grinned. "We've heard that story so many times."

"It's as vivid as if we actually lived it," Kathleen said.

Olvina said, "He's headed this way so the police are on the lookout for him."

After a pause long enough for all this to sink in, Wapinkino said, "Isn't Mr. Cameron in jail for a lot of crimes?"

"Serious crimes," Cassia said.

Olvina delivered the sad news. "Uncle Bradan said it's necessary to cancel all holiday leave and it will be rescheduled for another time, as well as days off. Every man and woman in this department will be on duty today. A notice was posted on the bulletin board at police headquarters so those that weren't in the information room at that time will also know. The ceremonies will draw a huge crowd. Just the kind of gathering criminals love to target."

"And what will the police be targeting?" Eunice said.

"Their objective is to bullseye any drugpushers and keep on the lookout for money and weapons," Olvina said. She paused and looked around at the faces of the others. "That's why I told Uncle Ken I would be backup for Uncle Bradan."

"And me," Phoebe added.

"With officers on holidays, there's a shortage and I want to help catch Mr. Cameron, and possibly Mr. Weistien, Sihon's father. Mr. Cameron is unlawfully out of jail and is dangerous. If you see either of these men, especially Mr. Cameron, don't approach him, call the police."

After that Olvina made her way across the lot to the dignitaries' box halfway down the length of one dock. She waved to the one of the women seated there. "Hello, Aunt Charlotte."

"Are Uncle Ken and Uncle Bradan waiting with the boat at the end of the dock?" Olvina asked.

"Yes, hurry," Charlotte answered.

Ken was the police chief superintendent. No one kept him waiting.

Olvina led the dash down the dock to where their uncles and Aunt Martha waited by the police boat. Her sisters, Wapinkino, and Trevor were right behind. Martha waited beside her husband Bradan. She held the position of public health nurse. She handed each teen a life preserver.

"Before climbing into the powerful police boat, slip on a life jacket," Martha said.

Trevor handed his life jacket back. "The boat will be crowded if we all go. I'll stay behind."

Wapinkino handed back his life preserver. "I'll stay behind with Trev."

The girls wriggled their way into their lifejackets.

"And zip it up." Cassia giggled.

The rest of the quints followed her example.

Soon the girls waited inside the boat, ready to push away from the dock.

Bradan undid the stern's rope.

He, too, was an impressive figure. In fine physical condition, his hair, also with graying sideburns, was dark brown and matched his eyes.

"Here you are, Olvina." Bradan leaped nimbly into positiob behind the dashboard and steering wheel.

Ken unwound the bow rope. "Phoebe, it's your job to see this rope is out of the way in the front of the boat."

The ease at which he worked showed he was used to working around boats and water. He either swam in the waters of Lake Forest, walked or boated with his life-long buddy, Bradan; and that's only when he wasn't playing sports with one of his five sons. It all helped keep his physique slim and tough, his reflexes honed.

Olvina hung onto the seat as the cruiser bounced over rough waters to the middle of the bay. Behind her in the next seat, Phoebe and Kathleen sat together. Kathleen sat on the inside seat clinging to the railing in order not to be thrown around. On the other side sat Cassia and Eunice.

Out here in the middle of the bay, the boat was more in line with the main body of the lake. The wind blew down it relatively unobstructed, even though there were lots of islands in the bay and closer to the shore.

Bradan stopped and idled the engine, then looked at Olvina. "This is the spot. Okay, go ahead. Do your part in the rescue dogs demonstration"

Eunice turned her head to listen to something on the shore.

Martin's voice reached them. "This rescue dog demonstration is about to start. The helicopter will be in the air as soon as the police boat moves away."

Olvina quickly stripped off her cadet uniform to the clothes she'd wear in the water. She sat at the edge of the boat, then tipped over backwards and landed in the water.

"Remember, you're unconscious in the cold water and can't help yourself," Bradan said.

Olvina thought of herself as a good swimmer and didn't necessarily need the life jacket, but she was glad she wore one once she felt herself being buffeted about by five-foot whitecaps.

Out of the corner of her eye, Olvina saw the helicopter rise into the air. The pilot did not start towards her immediately. In fact, he turned away, then circled the bay several times as if those on board were actually searching for someone.

She watched as the pilot banked and came towards her. Olvina lay with her head back, supported by the life jacket. The helicopter stopped and hovered above where the high waves tossed her around.

Olvina saw a huge grinning chocolate-colored labrador retriever and his handler waiting in the open doorway for the time to jump.

"Go," the man spoke to his dog with a downward sweep of his hand.

The brave animal leaped to the water several feet below the safety of the chopper, the handler following. They hit the waves with a tremendous splash, and without a pause, the dog, with one end of a lifeline in its mouth, swam towards her.

In the distance on shore, Olvina saw Martin and Martha stand to their feet as one, while the dog's trainer swam up to her. He tied an orange rope under her arms. The dog started swimming for shore.

Olvina felt a jerk as the dog hit the end of the line; she started to move.

Brave and strong, the retriever swam through five-foot waves, towing her and the handler. Only once the waves swept over them, but they surfaced immediately.

But the dog floundered.

For a brief second Olvina felt chilled. It wasn't the water that made her shiver either. For a brief second she wondered if the dog was strong enough to pull two people through such turbulence. Maybe I should let go of the rope? But she hung on.

The dog struggled then found his bearings. This time he made it to shore easily. He entered shallow water. His handler took Olvina in his arms and carried her to the sand and laid her down at and Martha's feet. She had her nurse's bag.

Martha said, "I need to examine you."

She felt Olvina's pulse and listened to her heart.

"You are in fine shape," she said.

Martha listened to Olvina's heart, then felt her pulse again.

"You are fine." She handed Olvina some clothes.

"Hurry and get into these dry garments before you catch a cold."

Chapter Two

After the search-and-rescue demonstration, the crowd watched a display of tandem horse jumping. Two officers rode their personal mounts over separate sets of jumps at the same time. The first one over the last jump won the event.

Olvina represented the Forest Lake Police detachment as a cadet. The horse she rode was a gentle bay mare. She came from the horse patrol unit which Morley Barclay headed along with the K9 unit.

The second rider came from the Lakeview detachment.

Phoebe joined Trevor and Wapinkino, who were sitting on the edge of the dock watching Olvina and her opponent on their way to the starting point. The two riders stopped by the dignitary box and Ken took a salute first from Olvina, then her co-rider.

The two horsemen were lined up at the starting gate.

The gun went off. The horses started out equally. Both horses took the first two jumps together. Olvina's horse faltered as she approached the next jump.

The mare stopped suddenly. Olvina plunged forward, almost spilling over the horse's head and onto the ground.

"Oh no," Phoebe and her friends moaned.

All joy drained from the group of teens. Kathleen covered her eyes with her hands. "Trouble at the third jump!"

Olvina didn't panic. Phoebe, Kathleen, Cassia and Eunice breathed easier when, calmly, she brought the mount under control, regrouped by making a wide arch then headed straight for the hurdle.

Phoebe cheered louder when the horse didn't refuse this time. Her sisters jumped up and down with relief beside her. Then hearts sank way low, as like a thunderbolt the Lakeview officer's mount picked up speed and seemed to fly down the stretch before the final jump.

"Will Olvina catch him in time?" Phoebe said.

Still calm, Olvina touched her horse with her heels; the horse leaped forward, covering the ground with sizzling speed.

"Go, go, go," Eunice cheered.

"Yeah for Olvina," Kathleen yelled.

"Faster," Trevor yelled. "Faster, Olvina, faster."

"You can beat the other rider," Wapinkino joined in.

Olvina's mare almost overtook the Lakeview horse. Both ran their horses stride-for-stride, neck-to-neck, nose-to-nose. This brought Phoebe, her group, and the rest of the spectators to their feet clapping, cheering, whistling, and making whatever noise they could, encouraging their favorite on.

Olvina asked for still more speed from her animal. The bay responded and left the ground to clear the final jump only by a mere fraction before her adversary's horse did.

Olvina won the event.

"This is where I leave you guys," Wapinkino said. "Mr. Turehue invited me to sing with him and Mr. Asquinn."

"I'll be real close in the seats, listening," Kathleen said.

"So will I," Cassia said.

"I love listening to The Gospel Singing Cops singing and playing," Eunice said.

Trevor and Phoebe rushed to Olvina as she swung down off her mount.

Trevor took the reins of the sweating horse from Olvina.

"I will walk her and cool her off, then let her drink and give her some oats."

"Sure thing."

From where the young people worked with the horse Olvina had ridden, the spectacular music awed Olvina. She set aside the brush she'd used on the mare and leaned against a railing, listening. With one foot resting on the bottom railing, Phoebe also leaned against the higher railings.

For the final event of July the First celebrations, Ken, Bradan, and Wapinkino, were on the stage playing fiddle tunes, singing, and would be there for the next three-quarters of an hour. This music didn't bring the crowd to their feet, instead they sat back, captivated by the music just as much as Olvina, Phoebe, and Trevor were.

None of the three paid any attention to anything else until the horse stomped her front feet and snorted.

Olvina turned to see what agitated her.

A voice spoke. "Hi, my friends."

"What?" Phoebe yelped.

Olvina turned to face the voice. "Wapinkino?" But, how could it be? He was still on stage singing? "Trev?"

But it was neither one she faced. It was Uncle Nigel Weistien that had spoken. Half-brother to Conrad Cameron. He was five-foot-ten inches, skinny and pale, his clothes hanging on him loosely.

Uncle Nigel wore a backwards baseball cap. Because of the cap neither girl nor Trevor could make out the color of the man's eyes, but guessed they were grayish blue.

"Who are you?" Trevor said.

"Oh, you know who I am."

"No, we don't," Phoebe squeaked. She cleared her throat. "No, we don't."

"So you two are part of the set of quintuplets I've heard so much about?" Nigel said.

"No, we're not," Olvina said.

"But you are. You can't fool me. The Asquinn quints."

"Who are you?" Olvina asked.

"Never mind who I am." With those words he quickly walked away and was gone.

Olvina stared after the spot she'd last seen him. She looked at Trevor, then Phoebe.

"You're trembling," Phoebe said.

"So are you," Olvina said. "Trev, don't you know who that is?"

"I sure do. He's Mr. Weistien, Sihon's father and Crystal's uncle before those two were adopted by Mr. and Mrs. Asquinn. I wanted him to think I didn't recognize him."

"And one of the men residence of Forest Lake had been warned to be on the lookout for," Olvina said.

"Should we report him to Uncle Ken or Uncle Bradan?" Phoebe asked.

"I think we ought to," Olvina said without hesitation.

Trevor agreed.

Just then the music from the stage swelled. Instead, the girls and Trevor resumed listening to the very two they should be explaining this strange meeting to play their violins and sing. All were hypnotized by the music and soon forgot about reporting the incident.

The two policemen and the Native youth played their signature tune. Olvina, Phoebe and Trevor rose to their feet along with the audience. They clapped and thumped until their voices were hoarse.

"More. More," Olvina shouted. Phoebe and Trevor joined in.

Olvina's voice was sore by the time the three played "The Orange Blossom Special" for an encore.

Olvina, her sister, and Trevor, made their way to the grandstand. Just before entering the area, she turned and looked towards four officers grouped together at the far end of the parking lot.

"Let's find out what they've turned up, if anything," she said.

"I don't think that's a good idea," Trevor said.

Olvina had started towards a thicket of trees that took her real close to the policemen.

Phoebe rolled her eyes in exasperation and followed. Trevor was right at her heels.

"Look at this, sir," Olvina heard an officer say to Bradan. He stood, along with three other officers, by a super sports car, its trunk open. The officers stepped aside to allow him to get closer to the car.

Olvina looked at her sister and cousin when their uncle let out a sharp breath after seeing what the trunk's contents consisted of.

"I wonder what it is?" Phoebe said.

"Drugs, maybe?" Trevor whispered.

"There must be close forty or fifty thousand dollars' worth of drugs there," Bradan said.

Along with the drug seizure, the girls saw the officers had six men handcuffed. Some were barely older than the sisters, Wapinkino, or

Trevor while others were maybe in their late twenties. They all appeared tough.

"Are you the chief superintendent?" one man asked Bradan. He gave Bradan a spiteful glare.

Bradan didn't tell him anything.

Olvina and Phoebe let out their breath; Trevor, too.

"It's really none of your business who I am." He looked at Morley. "Take those six and lock them up. You know what to do with these drugs."

Bradan turned and strode back to the grandstand and joined Martha.

Olvina sprang to her feet and started running towards the stands, Trevor right behind her. Phoebe was right behind him.

In the grandstand, Ken had already started the ceremony.

Olvina joined the rest of her sisters and the boys. They listened intently as he talked, totally absorbed in his speech.

"I will try and keep my words short. I want to welcome each and every one of you into the Forest Lake Provincial detachment. I'm confident all four of you will make fine policemen. I want to assure you I'm behind all four of you as long as your actions bring honor to this department.

"Today, you are about to receive diplomas. You should be proud of these, as they are symbols of what you've accomplished over the past few months, and also are the start of not a new chapter, but a new book in your lives. May God be with you in this unceasing and ever-growing hot fight against crime. Believe me, you will often need His help in this endeavor. Now for the diplomas." He picked up a piece of paper from a tall little table in front of him.

"I'll start at the back of the alphabet. Constable, Turehue Lyle."

Lyle, nineteen years old, was Bradan and Martha's youngest son. They had two more daughters.

Olvina and her sisters watched. Her heart swelled with pride, as Lyle stepped in front of his uncle and received his diploma. Then after a snappy salute, which Ken returned, he stepped back in line.

Olvina clapped and cheered. Encouragement flowed from her. The noisy cheering continued on throughout the ceremony.

"Constable, Turehue Gerald," Ken said.

Gerald, at twenty-two, was oldest of the family, and a mirror image of his father, Chief Inspector Bradan Turehue. Gerald received his diploma.

Ken continued on, ending up with the letter A. "Constable, Asquinn Kirk."

Ken's second eldest stepped in front of him. Following the trend of his two cousins, he received the diploma and then it was his older brother's turn.

A hush fell over the crowd.

"Constable, Asquinn Murray." The eldest stepped forward and stood before his father, also a mirror image of his elder.

"Congratulations, son. Be proud of your diplomas, all four of you. It's a symbol of the milestone you've passed today, and wear your uniform with pride and do nothing to disgrace it."

Ken handed his son his diploma. Murray took the paper, saluted, and stepped back into line with his brother and cousins.

"And now for food and refreshments," Ken said to the crowd.

Gerald and Lyle went to their father and mother, the girls' Uncle Bradan and Aunt Martha. There were a lot of hugs and congratulations exchanged, especially as Murray, Kirk, Ken and Charlotte joined in.

Olvina and Kathleen joined Martin, Audrey, Sihon, and Crystal. Sihon went to the tables laden with food. Ahead of her sisters, Olvina eyed what was set in front of them: cold meat cuts, potatoes and gravy, salad and a buttered bun cut in half.

Trevor touched Olvina's elbow and signaled for her to follow.

"Trevor wants us to go with him," Olvina said to Martin. Martin nodded. Olvina led the way to where some cousins and friends filled their plates.

"Oh, boy, real food," Crystal said.

The group filled their plates with sloppy joes, chili dogs and pizza, and under this burden of food, made their way to the dining tents and found a table. Olvina was thankful the tent was situated close to the lake so received plenty of the breeze, keeping the pesky mosquitoes away.

Olvina and Phoebe started eating the delicious food, but had barely swallowed their first bite of pizza when Bradan pulled a chair away from the table nearest the two cadets and sat down.

Olvina said, "This is the end of school for Murray, Kirk, Lyle and Gerald. Now they will take orders from their chief inspector. Even though he may be their father or uncle, he is also their commanding officer."

"Yes," Bradan said.

"What will the four graduates do now? Start work immediately?"

"No, not immediately. They have a few days before they come on duty. Unless an emergency pops up. How often do we have one of them here? How do you feel now that the excitement is all over?"

"I can't wait to get started helping you fight the bad guys in this community."

Their uncle said with a big smile, "Good, then you can come down to headquarters with me. I'll show you what your schedule will be."

"But..."

"No buts. We have our duties to perform. Now!" Bradan's tone warned Olvina or Phoebe not to argue. Olvina began to wonder if she would adjust to the strict discipline that being a policeman demanded.

Olvina looked at the plate full of food. "Yes, sir." She, then Phoebe, pushed back their chairs and prepared to leave along with their uncle. But the sisters saw he wasn't ready to go yet, and remained seated.

He turned to his partner, Ken.

"Ken, there's stuff down at the station you have to see. And I need to fill you in on what took place here during the festivities."

"All right, if it's that urgent," Ken said.

Olvina and Phoebe exchanged astonished looks at Ken's reply. It wasn't often Ken allowed any of his underlings to drag him away on his days off. Olvina swallowed some of her food, and Kathleen sneaked another bite from her pizza.

Ken pushed back his chair and stood. So did Bradan. So did Olvina and Phoebe. They all paused to take leave of their wives and families.

Ken bent over and kissed his wife beside him at the table. "Duty calls, dear."

Charlotte said, "Yes dear, I know. I've been a policeman's wife long enough to know."

Bradan talked to someone on his radio. "We're coming down immediately. Have today's seizure of goods on display. Come on, Olvina, Phoebe."

He turned his attention to the rest of the group. "Cassia, Phoebe, Eunice, Trev, Wapinkino, you might as well go home, the First of July Festivities are breaking up. Get some rest for duty tonight, Trev, Wapinkino."

"Uncle Bradan, Wapinkino isn't a volunteer cadet," Trevor said.

Bradan bent down to kiss Martha.

"Good-bye for now, dear," Martha said.

On their way, the group passed Martin's table. Olvina and Phoebe quickly said good-bye to him and Audrey.

***

Olvina and Phoebe walked along with their uncles the quarter mile to police headquarters. Bradan paused on the corridor inside the place.

He stood aside and swept his arm inside the room. "After you," he said.

Phoebe followed Olvina, who was right behind Ken, into the evidence room. Bradan entered last.

Olvina and Phoebe's gaze fell on rows upon rows of seized weapons and drugs. Some drugs were done up in plastic bags while others were wrapped in brown wrapping paper. Like his second in command before him, Ken drew in a deep breath.

Olvina exchanged a look of astonishment with her sister. Both realized the scope of this drug bust.

Beside Olvina, Phoebe gulped as Ken picked up one of the weapons and examined it, then set it back it its place. "Anyone arrested?"

"Yes, six men," Bradan said. "I didn't tell you about this before they were jailed because one man asked me if I was the superintendent. All six looked tough and ready to kill at a moment's notice, but this man particularly so. I pretended I didn't know what he was talking about. I felt it was a good idea to tell officers to get those six men away from the ceremonies and jail them."

"Well done," Ken said. "Steller job, my friend."

"I think this hashish has been imported into Canada from southwest Asia to help finance the terrorists," Bradan said.

"And you would be right," said Ken. "It will be your job to find out who's behind the distribution in this area. Sorry, but I won't be around to help out for a few weeks. I start my holidays, once Morley's back, but if I'm needed, I'll be available until then. You are free to go on patrol now."

Olvina and Phoebe walked on either side of their uncle to the cruiser.

By the time the shift ended at four o'clock in the afternoon, all three were tired.

Olvina and Phoebe were willing to go home when Kathleen and Cassia's shift started. Eunice and Trevor would be assisting on night shift.

Chapter Three

Early the next morning, Olvina opened her eyes. She glanced at Crystal on the last bed in the row of six. Her chest rose up and down in sleep. Kathleen and Cassia were also asleep in their beds. The remaining bed was empty; Eunice would be on duty. Turning over on her side, she glanced at the hands of the clock hanging right in the middle of the flowery wall-papered room. Five o'clock AM. She glanced at the calendar. It was Monday, July 18, 1978.

Olvina kicked back the covers, jumped silently to the floor and crept over to Crystal's bed. She lightly touched her sister's shoulder then shook her

"Huh? Wh...what?"

"Time to get up if you wanna see Uncle Ken, Aunt Charlotte and our cousins off."

Everyone woke up in an instant. "Oh yeah."

Olvina slipped out of the room and into the washroom to freshen up. Phoebe wanted the use of the room just as Olvina brushed the last stroke through her hair. Olvina went downstairs. Only Sihon moved. They waited for their sisters in the kitchen.

"Wait for us," Martin called from the master bedroom.

After, they joined the children.

"I hope Ken and Charlotte haven't left yet," Martin said.

"Let's hurry."

"Uncle Ken wanted to get an early start on his vacation," Olvina said. She led the way outside.

The young people started running towards their uncle's place. As they trooped into the yard, and joined the other well-wishers there, Ken helped Charlotte into the cab of the thirty-foot camper.

Ken greeted Martin and Audrey. "Good morning." Then said to the children, "You kids are up early."

"We wanted to see you off, Uncle Ken, Aunt Charlotte," Olvina said.

"And wish you all a happy holiday," Crystal said.

"Why, thank you," Charlotte said gratefully.

"I'm sure we will have a nice holiday," Ken said.

Bradan, with Martha at his side, stepped up to Ken.

"Bradan, my friend, I'm handing command of the Forest Lake Police Department over to you while I'm holidays."

"Thank you. I will keep the department running smoothly while you are away," Bradan said.

Ken followed his three younger sons—Brian, Raymond and Syd—aboard, and took the seat behind the steering wheel.

Martha and all the well-wishers waved as he backed the camper down the driveway and onto the street, turned towards the west part of Forest Lake and the big highway, and slowly started moving along Golden Ridge Circle Drive. Soon the camper was out of sight.

Sad, Olvina turned away. They headed homeward again.

***

That evening, their shift over, Olvina and Phoebe accompanied Wapinkino. Dusk had already arrived and they escorted him home from where he hung out a fair amount with Owen.

"It's nice to be on my way home after a long day," Wapinkino said.

"We enjoy walking you home," Olvina said.

Olvina exchanged a look with her sister. The two smiled knowingly, aware Wapinkino preferred Kathleen to be among them walking with him.

"Did Mr. Turehue assign you to walk me home as part of police cadet duty?' Wapinkino asked.

"Oh no," Phoebe assured him. "It's late in the evening and we simply wanted to see you arrive home safely."

"We've done this done since you started working volunteer for Mr. Winschell," Olvina said.

Wapinkino said with a break in his voice, "Thanks."

Phoebe shrugged off their friend's sentiments. "It's the least we can do."

"I'm doing this for you, a friend," Olvina said.

The three friends rounded the curve across the valley from the farm where Mr. Chester Greene, an authentic Forest Lake resident, lived at one time. He'd been moved recently to an apartment in Forest Lake village.

Suddenly Wapinkino grew serious. "Let's hurry home. I have a bad feeling."

They traveled down one side of the valley, came up the other side in front of the farmhouse where Morley and Gay-Anne Barclay bought the property and now lived there. Gay-Anne's last name before marrying had been Asquinn, which made her, the girls' and Sihon first cousins. Morley was a cousin by marriage.

Instead of following the curvature of the road around the ridge, Olvina climbed the gate and scrambled down the other side.

"I hope Morley or Gay-Anne didn't see us doing that," Wapinkino said as he landed on the packed dirt on the other side beside Olvina and Phoebe.

Wapinkino led the way as fast as their legs could carry them through the tall grass.

He led the way through the yard of a summer cabin right next door to Eric Asquinn, another of the quint's uncles, down the driveway to the road then turned onto the railway crossing.

On the bottom of the little railroad embankment there was a small parking spot where fishermen from all over parked to fish in Lake Forest. From there, tracks worn in the soft ground from horses and wagons hauling supplies in earlier years when Forest Lake was a thriving mining town were etched into the ground. The tracks followed an open space between trees for a while. The tracks came to a creek. The area would be overly wet in spring thaw. To fight this, small trees had been cut from the surrounding forest and placed to form a corduroy bridge. No one had driven over the trail since Mr. Olson bought the house Wapinkino's family now lived in. No one but Mr. Olson would know the roadway was now dry enough to drive over.

Suddenly, Wapinkino stopped and stared, his eyes focused on the truck tire marks on the crude road.

"Do you know who it could be?" Phoebe said.

"I have a pretty good idea."

"Your dad?"

The dark youth nodded.

"What do you think?" Olvina said.

"I don't know. Dad's visits with Mom have always ended with Mom in tears and him storming out in a rage. Why should this one be different?"

"Trust God this visit will be special," Olvina said.

Wapinkino continued along a footpath through the woods and to his house. This trail was the shortest of the three shortcuts. On the other side of a narrow band of trees waves lapped gently upon the shoreline. The moon reflected bright and silver off the surface of Wan Asquinn, a bay of Lake Forest.

Wapinkino and his brothers and sisters used this trail since it was midsummer and the flood areas were dried up.

Olvina fell in behind him, Phoebe behind her. Like the Snow Owl—the meaning of his dark youth's name in his native language—Wapinkino glided silently and accurately along the narrow dirt footpath. Lake Forest flooded every year during the spring break up, but it was late enough in the summer for the trail to be dry. They crossed the little stream at the end of Wan Asquinn without incident.

On the south side of the stream was a summer residence. The grass around the cabin was neat and trim and lots of footprints dotted the beach only yards away. The family wasn't at home now. They mostly came out only on weekends. During the week the father worked.

A little further down stood another cabin.

Olvina, Phoebe and Wapinkino walked on by.

They stopped in front of Wapinkino's house.

"We're coming in," Olvina said.

This caused Wapinkino to do something he'd never done before, shocking both girls. He turned on them. "No, you are most certainly not. It's late. Go home now and I will see you tomorrow."

After those words, Wapinkino chased the girls away from the front steps, not allowing either into the house.

He went inside.

Once the door closed behind him, Olvina turned to her sister and touched her shoulder. When she had Phoebe's attention, she pointed to where a truck sat parked. Olvina crouched low so as to be very careful not to be seen as they circled the vehicle. Olvina stopped at the front license plate. Phoebe stopped inches from her shoulder.

Olvina whispered to her. "Whatever we do, we must be sure to remember the license plate number."

"What for?"

Olvina didn't answer. Instead she pointed towards the house and the living room window, which provided a panoramic view of Lake Forest. The drapes were open and screen windows let in the cool night breezes. Phoebe immediately understood Olvina's intentions and nodded.

"I don't see Wapinkino."

With Phoebe following, Olvina started towards the shadowy area in some bushes below the window. They approached the front window using brush and flowers as cover, and got close enough to peek inside.

Olvina gestured to her sister and pointed. "I see him."

"Where?"

"See, by the kitchen door. He's talking to his father."

Phoebe looked in that direction and nodded, signaling Olvina she saw their friend, too.

Wapinkino said something, but neither Olvina nor Phoebe heard him.

There was no electricity in this house as the hydro lines did not come this far. Black surrounded the house now and the forest close by. Only dim lamp light lit up the inside of the house.

Nervousness chilled Olvina. Beside her, Phoebe trembled.

Phoebe jumped back from the window. Olvina put a hand over her sister's mouth to silence a shout.

"That is not a typical domestic scene," Phoebe croaked when Olvina released her.

Mrs. Olson clung to Wapinkino where they sat together on a couch. Mr. Olson perched on the back of the sofa, arguing with his wife. Mrs. Olson looked frightened and in tears.

Olvina touched Phoebe's shoulder with her fingers to get her attention. "Look, in that easy chair by the fireplace."

Phoebe looked. "Isn't that Uncle Conrad Cameron?"

"Yes. It's clear he's in control and has the Olson family subdued with fear."

"You mean with that shotgun across his lap?" Phoebe whispered back.

"And the empty cans of soft drinks on an end table and Uncle sipping from one in his hand," Olvina said.

Olvina looked around one more time. She said, "I don't see any of the younger children."

"They must be asleep," Phoebe said.

Olvina backed away from the window. Phoebe did the same.

"This is clearly a family being held hostage," Olvina said.

"Why Mr. Olson? What part does he play in this drama?" Phoebe asked.

Olvina noticed Conrad get up from his chair, walk over to the side door, and open it. Holding onto Wapinkino, he stepped out onto the top stoop and looked around. Wapinkino was with the man, but he didn't seem to be going along willingly.

Olvina's eyes followed the two. Conrad walked down the step. He pushed the youth ahead of him. He walked to the spot where the girls had been seconds before.

"I don't think Uncle Conrad's looking for evidence of anyone being there," Olvina whispered.

"He's stopped to light up a cigarette," Phoebe said in a low voice.

"He's holding something in his hand."

"What is it?"

"It's a small pistol, and he's holding it to Wapinkino's side," Olvina said. "Great. A hostage taker under the influence of some kind of drug. Oh man, what an explosive situation. This night could erupt into anything."

Conrad put out whatever it was he was smoking and went inside, pushing his hostage ahead of him.

As one, Olvina and Phoebe turned and fled. Using the stars for light, Olvina led the dash back along the trail they'd travelled earlier towards home.

The girls were still in the shadows at the bottom of the railroad crossing below Golden Ridge where the church their grandfather pastored stood. Olvina came to a sudden stop. Phoebe crashed into her.

"Oh!" Olvina yelped, frightened and backed off.

"What's the matter?" Phoebe whispered.

"I don't know. I can see something but can't recognize what it is."

In the light of the moon, Olvina noticed Phoebe's eyes shone with fear. Terror filled Olvina from the roots of her hair to the tips of her toes.

"Oh no," Phoebe groaned. "Now we're truly dead. One of those gang members will capture us and drag us into whatever's going on at Wapinkino's."

Olvina moved closer to her sister, who stood frozen to one spot, frightened. Both girls heard a snicker.

Chapter Four

"I recognize that snicker," Phoebe said, relieved.

"Wait a minute. Don't be afraid. It's me," said a cheery voice.

"Uncle Bradan," both girls squealed.

"Why are you running? You ran as if you thought someone bad back there at Olson's was going to jump out and grab you. What are you talking about? Dead? Gang members?" he said.

When neither Olvina nor Phoebe answered, he continued. "And what's this about what's going on over there? What's spooked you two?"

"Are you on foot? Alone?" Olvina asked. "You aren't in uniform. I remember, you are off duty."

Bradan rubbed his hands together. "Ahhhhhh, so you can talk. Tell me more."

Olvina fearfully looked back over her shoulder and noticed Olson's windows were still lit up by coal oil lamp light.

Bradan followed her gaze. "Isn't that a bit unusual for so many lights to be on at their place so late at night?"

"That's what Phoebe and I thought," Olvina said. "There was a truck parked in front of Olson's place when he came home from work. It's still there."

"Wapinkino seemed uneasy about it all, too," Phoebe added. Then, "Uncle Bradan, I'm scared."

"I can see that. Why should you be scared about Olson's having visitors?"

"Can we go inside?" Olvina asked.

"Sure," Uncle Bradan said. "I'll walk you two home. It's past your curfew."

The three made the short walk to Martin's.

Martin, Audrey, Eunice, Crystal, and Sihon were in the front room talking when Bradan arrived home with his charges. Cassia and Kathleen would be helping Morley police Forest Lake until midnight.

When Martin saw Olvina and Phoebe in the doorway of the living room with Bradan he gave his wife a worried glance.

Olvina looked at Phoebe.

Martin rose to his feet and came to the door, greeted him with a warm smile. "Why hello, Bradan. Come on in and be seated, please."

"Sorry about this unexpected visit,"

"You are always welcome here," Martin said.

"Hi, Uncle Bradan," Eunice said.

"Hi, Uncle Bradan," Crystal said.

"Hi, Uncle Bradan," Sihon said.

Bradan returned the greetings.

He lowered himself into an armchair. "Olvina and Phoebe have come to me with a complaint."

"We didn't exactly go to him," Olvina said.

"We just bumped into him," Phoebe said.

Olvina hoped their parents didn't notice them trembling.

She hoped her sisters and brothers didn't notice either. Sihon must have because after looking the quints' and Crystal's way, he put a hand to his mouth to stifle a giggle.

Bradan turned to Olvina and Phoebe. "Now, tell me, what has you spooked?"

Olvina stood and walked over to one of the windows that faced towards Olson's across the bay. She pulled back a corner of the curtain and looked across the water to their friend's place. "Every house but Olson's is dark," she said.

"You have to distract Uncle Bradan for a possible domestic dispute?" Sihon said.

"Shut up, Sihon," Eunice said and slapped him with a couch cushion.

"It hasn't got anything to do with that," Olvina said.

"Then what?" their uncle wanted to know. His tone indicated he'd just received a premonition about something terrible. "Tell me quick."

"We have a feeling something's going on over there that shouldn't be," Olvina said.

Phoebe's voice shook with fear. "The place is all lit up. And it's so quiet; no body's moving around."

Sihon, Crystal, and Eunice exchanged amused looks.

"How foolish and imaginary," Eunice said. "Olvina, Phoebe, don't be f—"

"Shush," Bradan said. He fished a pen and notebook from his shirt pocket. "I looked over at Olson's house before coming inside. You girls are right. There is something strange going on over there."

Olvina watched him write in bold, black letters on top of the page:06/20/1968 11:00 O'clock AM

When Bradan looked up from his writing, he reached out and touched Olvina's hair. "I'll go over there but first I want to know why you feel there's something going on?"

"It's the weirdest feeling, Uncle Bradan," Olvina said.

"It came over both of us when we were coming home from Wapinkino's," Phoebe said.

"We have reason to believe Mister—" Phoebe stopped and glanced from Sihon to Crystal "Someone is holding the Olson family hostage."

These words brought Bradan straight up in his chair. They also caught the attention of all in the room.

"Why?" He said.

"We saw him in a chair with a shotgun placed on his lap," Phoebe said.

"You mentioned a truck. Can you describe the truck?" Bradan said.

"It's a half ton, kinda an older model as it was quite dented and battered," Phoebe said.

"It's a two-tone brown color," Olvina said.

"No, it isn't. The truck is a solid light brown," Phoebe said.

Bradan wrote all this down, then said, "You two are very observant if you noticed all those details. Did you notice the license plate? Was it an Ontario plate or out-of-province plate?"

"I didn't notice," Olvina said.

"Me neither," Phoebe said.

"Never mind. I'll find out when I go over there."

"What's the description of a beat-up old truck got to do with Wapinkino's safety?" Sihon asked.

"It might have a lot to do with it," said Bradan.

"Is Nadine okay, Uncle Bradan?" Crystal asked. "Nadine is my friend. We're in the same grade at school."

"I know, honey. Olson's are fine," Bradan assured the youngest.

Olvina saw understanding of what might be happening spread across Martin's face, nor was she surprised when he asked, "Do you think the truck belongs to Mr. Olson?"

"Wapinkino didn't say it was his father's; he only assumed it was," Olvina said.

"He wouldn't allow us inside the house. Instead, he told us to go home," Phoebe said.

"Bradan, do you think Mr. Olson would hurt the family if it is him?" Audrey said.

Uncle Bradan looked grim. "I can't say at this time. Domestic situations do have a way of turning violent."

He looked from Olvina to Phoebe. "Did you see anyone else? Did you see Wapinkino after he went into the house? Or hear any noises, like someone screaming?"

"A tall, blond man argued with Mrs. Olson." Suddenly Olvina's mind went blank and she couldn't recall anymore.

Phoebe picked up the story. "We got out of there as fast as we could. The last we saw of Wapinkino was when he left us to go inside."

Bradan took notes. He didn't speak until he finished. When he looked up, he spoke calmly to Olvina and Phoebe, but included every kid in the room. "I'm certain it's nothing. You young ones go to bed now."

At that instant, Cassia, then Kathleen, burst through the back entrance. Morley and Trevor followed.

"I'm so tired," Kathleen said.

"I'm so glad that shift is over," Cassia said.

"Morley, Eunice and Trevor will take over now," Bradan said.

Eunice rose to her feet. She went out into the night with her cousins. A cruiser engine started outside, then drifted away.

Olvina was the first to hug Martin and Audrey, and even Uncle Bradan.

"Good night, Dad, Mom, Uncle Bradan."

"Good night," Audrey said and hugged her daughters.

Olvina started towards the stairs to her room on the upper part of the house. Sihon just had to cross the living room to his sleeping place. He went inside and shut the door.

"Be sure to get some sleep now," Bradan called after the disappearing youths.

The sisters didn't even prepare for bed. Olvina lay on her side, her arm on the pillows, bent at the elbow, her head resting on one hand. Kathleen lay at the end of the row on her back. She held her hands behind her head. All five were quiet.

When silence came from the upper part of the house, Olvina heard Martin say, "Something serious is going on, isn't it?"

Olvina couldn't see the adults in the living room or even see all the way down the stairs. The girls had neglected to close the door to their room and Olvina could make out what their dad said, and the conversation that followed. Once Olvina glanced down the line of sisters. She knew they'd heard also.

"We received a bit of news via the Internet," Bradan said. "Conrad escaped from prison about three weeks ago."

"Oh, no!" five pairs of listening ears heard Audrey gasp.

"We watched it on the news recently," Martin said.

"Does Sihon know his uncle escaped from jail?" Uncle Bradan asked.

"No," Martin answered. "Neither does Crystal know anything about her father's escape. Should we tell him?"

"It's up to you," Uncle Bradan said.

"How did he do that? I thought he was in a maximum security prison?" Audrey said.

"He was. He knew enough to behave himself. New prisoners were brought in and the officials declared the prison overcrowded. The old ones that had chalked up a record of good behavior had to be moved to a prison with more relaxed security."

"And Conrad was among them?" Martin said.

"Right," Bradan replied. "He was put on a work crew. One day, while the guards were busy at something else, he simply walked away from the group."

Bradan paused.

Upstairs in their room, Olvina moved to the end of the bed, eager to hear more. Kathleen moved to Olvina, Cassia's, and Phoebe's bed in order to hear better as well.

"We thought he was headed this way," Bradan said. "There were reports of groceries being stolen from the backs of trucks then the other bags tipped over and scattered about, perhaps to make the owners think ravens had raided the supplies. And clothes had been stolen from clotheslines."

A chair creaked.

"He must be leaving," Olvina whispered, as more shuffling reached their ears.

Footsteps. Their voices grew faint.

Olvina jumped to the floor and hurried to the landing outside the bedroom door. Her sisters joined her and crouched in a line beside her as she listened.

"Once I'm out, lock the door, and don't open it to anyone but me—or any policeman you know."

The outside door opened and closed.

"I knew it," Olvina said.

"Something very serious is going on," Kathleen added.

Footsteps as someone reentered the kitchen.

Then they paused.

"How long have you been in the doorway of your room?" Martin asked. His voice sounded angry.

Sure they'd been discovered and in for a reprimand, Olvina, followed by her sisters, stood and fled back to their room and were under the covers in no time, still fully dressed. Crystal was already in bed and asleep.

"Not long, Dad," Sihon's voice faintly reached the girls. "I just now got up for a drink of water."

"Hurry and get your drink of water," Audrey said, "then we will all get our sleep."

After the house grew quiet, Olvina changed into her bed clothes.

Crystal climbed up beside Olvina's bed. "I'm scared, Olvina. Is something bad happening?"

Olvina drew the younger girl into her arms and hugged her.

"Nothing the police can't handle. Uncle Bradan and his help will protect us."

"With God's help," Cassia spoke from her bed.

"Can I sleep with you?" Crystal asked.

"You sure can," Olvina said. She made room for her to get into the bed. They snuggled together and soon all were asleep. They slept soundly.

***

After Bradan left Martin's place, he went straight across the narrow alley between his and Ken's to home.

"I have to go to work," he told Martha. "Conrad has the Olson family as hostages in their own house."

"Oh my," Martha gasped.

She went to the closet where Bradan stored his uniforms and guns. She handed him a fresh uniform. After changing, he armed his belt with his gun and nightstick.

At the door, Martha looked into her husband's eyes.

"I hate sending you away like this," she said. "I have no way of knowing if I will see you again in a few hours or in a few days."

She kissed Bradan. "I'll be praying for your safety."

She watched as he walked out into the calm night.

***

Olvina and Phoebe worked with their uncle on the day shift. Bradan and his helpers were stationed outside the Olson house.

"What do you want, Conrad?"

"You're Bradan?"

"That's right."

"Where's your boss?"

"You mean my partner Ken? He's holidaying."

"Holidaying, is he? Well, you'd better get him back here because I refuse to talk to anyone but him."

Bradan tried reasoning with the madman, but Conrad only laughed at him.

"Why, Bradan, you're a trained cop. With all the modern technology, you could locate him in three hours."

"Maybe, maybe not."

"It's best you try," Conrad said. He suddenly let Mrs. Olson go but grabbed the baby from her arms. The baby cried right away.

What Conrad said next made the sisters' blood curdle.

"If you don't, I'll kill this baby!"

But Bradan wasn't fazed. "I don't believe that for an instant, Conrad."

"Believe it. I'll smash her head against this cement pillar if you don't start working this instant on locating your boss."

"I'm not going to track down Ken," Bradan said. "He's on vacation. He left me in charge. It's up to me how things are run from now on until he comes back off holidays. What do you want?"

"I want my daughter, Crystal, back. I won't let this family go until you meet my demands." With those parting words, Conrad returned inside the house and closed the door.

"I feel dread for the future of the Olson babies, Uncle Bradan," Olvina said when Conrad and Mrs. Olson were out of sight.

Bradan talked on the two-way radio, trying to rouse Morley.

"Please answer right away," Olvina said.

On the first ring, she heard a sleepy voice.

"Hello, Morley speaking."

Bradan said, "I need help immediately. Get dressed and meet me by the second summer residence closest to Olson's."

"I'm there already," Morley answered.

Bradan ended the call. He immediately dialed another number and the dispatcher at headquarters answered on the first ring.

Bradan spoke quietly into the microphone. "I need backup. I'm on the lawn between the two cottages by Olson's."

"What's going on?"

Bradan said urgently, "Conrad is back. Lawrence Olson is back. The Olson family has been taken hostage. I want every officer down here fast! It doesn't matter if they're sleeping, on days off or about to start their holidays. Get everyone down here!"

"I'm on it, sir."

"And make sure there are no sirens, no lights." Bradan ended the call.

Morley had already arrived. Murray, Kirk, Gerald, and Lyle arrived shortly after him. Two police cruisers were parked by the cottages.

Chapter Five

"Quick! We have to evacuate every house from Pastor Asquinn's, Eric's, Tim's and Bradley's, and that house on the ridge east of here," Bradan said urgently. "See if there's anyone in the house. If there is, see that they seek shelter with Gay-Anne. That way your wife, Morley, won't be alone. And all of you make sure no lights are turned on. Go!"

"Yes, sir," Morley said. He strode towards Uncle Eric's back door. Gerald went to Uncle Tim's, and Kirk went to Uncle Bradley's and his family.

Olvina remained very happily at Bradan's side. So did Phoebe.

Bradan headed towards the road through Forest Lake, then around the corner to Martin's house, Olvina and Phoebe with him. He knocked at the back door. Martin opened it. He didn't seem surprised to see Bradan, or his two daughters. But Phoebe's serious face seemed to alarm him. Audrey joined her husband.

"Lyle was just here," Martin said. "Eric's bringing his family here. Mom and Dad are also staying here."

"I'm sorry," Bradan said, "but I must ask you not to turn on any lights and try not to alarm the kids."

The evacuees started arriving. Pastor Asquinn and the first of the children filed into the kitchen. Eric held a position in the middle. Martha and the pastor's wife walked at the back of the line.

"Hurry, Shannon, Joanne. Keep up with the others," Martha said.

Bradan, Olvina, and Phoebe helped Martha and Mrs. Asquin swiftly usher in the children and four adults into the living room.

"Try and keep as quiet as possible, please" Bradan said as the newcomers joined the rest of the quints and found places to settle down. "This evening keep the lights dim, and stay away from the windows."

Bradan turned to Martin and Audrey and said, "And keep a close watch on Sihon and Crystal."

"We won't let them out of our sight," Martin said.

In the house, Martha secretly kept an eye on Olvina and Phoebe. Both trembled from fright and seemed to be trying to hide it from the adults, especially Bradan.

Bradan turned to look at Olvina, then Phoebe. "Cassia and Kathleen are on duty now; it's four o'clock in the afternoon."

At home Olvina started up the stairs to the girls' room. Another day.

***

The next morning Olvina had just finished brushing her teeth when there was a knock on the door.

"That will be Morley. He's here to escort you girls to where Uncle Bradan awaits," Martin said.

By the time Morley, Olvina and Phoebe reached Olson's property the entire region from the railroad crossing at the tip of Golden Ridge to all the way around Olson's had been cordoned off.

Behind the police tape, in the yards between the two cabins, Bradan set up a command area. Standing by one of the cruisers, he lifted a loud speaker to his lips. "Conrad, we have the house surrounded. Surrender, or we'll come in and get you."

Murray, Kirk, Gerald and Lyle moved towards the side entrance of the house. Conrad appeared in the doorway, holding a shotgun in his arms, Mrs. Olson close to him, an infant in her arms.

Conrad fired one round from the shotgun. Bradan, Olvina and Phoebe cringed.

"He shot out the cabin's front window," Bradan said. "Go back."

His son, Gerald, led the retreat for cover. Uncle Bradan found safety behind a cruiser, Olvina and Phoebe with him.

Conrad called out in a loud voice, "What are you going to do now?

Are you going to send them in after me again? If you do I won't be shooting at front windows."

***

The next morning Olvina ran the brush through her long sandy colored hair as she got ready for another shift. She used her parents' bathroom downstairs as Phoebe had been busy in the upstairs one tidying up for the day. She desecended the stairs.

The phone on the wall outside the kitchen rang.

Phoebe took down the receiver from its cradle. "Hello, Phoebe speaking."

"Phoebe, my girl, I need your and Olvina's assistance. Come on over to the crime scene immediately. We are going for a helicopter ride."

"We'll be there in five minutes, Uncle Bradan."

"You will be here in three minutes," Bradan said in a no-nonsense tone, then more gently, "Trevor and Eunice are about to end their shift."

Phoebe put the receiver down and was out of the house in record time even for her. Olvina followed.

Later, in the helicopter, Olvina shaded her eyes with one hand and looked to the east. The pilot, Morley, turned the chopper towards what would be Barclay's home fields. Soon the chopper flew above the valley behind their house.

Olvina estimated where the pilot would land and watched Morley bring the chopper down next to some dog kennel buildings and training fields hidden from public view on lower-level fields. Here she, Phoebe and the police officers climbed to the ground.

"How is your police dog training program coming?" Phoebe inquired.

They approached some runs built into both sides of the building. Three dogs filled the runs at one end. One wagged his whole body at Morley's approach.

"Good," Morley said.

Morley strode to the door of the run. The lock made a clinking sound as he pulled the pin; he opened the door and allowed Valiant his freedom. The huge animal stood on his hind legs and rested his paws affectionately on his owner's shoulders. He stood higher than his handler.

"This is Valiant. He's the Shiloh Shepherd I've trained for police work."

"He's so huge," Phoebe said. "He resembles a German Shepherd."

"But stunningly handsome," Olvina said. She knelt and ran her fingers through the dogs shiny grey hair. Phoebe became brave enough to pet the dog behind the ears.

"All he needs now is some real police work to see if he has what it takes to start a K-9 unit," Morley said.

"You never know. Maybe he will find the test he needs before this is over," Olvina said.

Shiloh Shepherds had the same characteristics as a German Shepherd, also the same features, but Shiloh Shepherds weighed one hundred and sixty pounds and grew to about thirty-one inches at the shoulder.

Olvina and Phoebe, along with the two policemen, and the dog, dashed across the meadow and into the house.

If Gay-Anne was surprised to see the men and two teen-aged cadets and a wolf-sized dog suddenly burst through the door into her kitchen, she didn't say anything. Raised in a police family, she was used to the unusual, it seemed.

"We'll be staying here to get a good rest," Morley told her, "before continuing on down to the siege area."

***

Later that afternoon, Bradan pushed away his empty ice cream dish.

"Ahhh," he said with great delight. "I've managed to complete a meal at last. Thank you, Gay. Excuse us while Morley, Olvina, Phoebe and I talk in the living room."

Bradan pushed back his chair. The girls and Morley followed his movements. Everyone followed him to the livingroom.

From the kitchen came noises of Gay-Anne clearing the table. There was a silence.

Bradan's face grew solemn.

His nieces looked at him.

"He wants Crystal back," Olvina said.

"He tried to get you to trace Uncle Ken by threatening to kill the

Olson baby girls," Phoebe said.

"He really is coming undone, isn't he?" Bradan said.

Olvina thought he remained calm and didn't appear worried at all.

"Phoebe and I think he's also on drugs," Olvina said.

"Do you know what kind?" Morley asked.

Phoebe shook her head.

"We saw him drinking out of a soft drink can," Olvina said. "Could've been laced with something. He was also smoking something."

"Could it have just been an ordinary cigarette?" Bradan said.

Olvina shook her head. "Kind of an odd shape for that. Looked more like a joint."

Morley's forehead crinkled in thought. "He could be high for days if he continues if he has enough of a supply to keep using the drug. Has he shown any tendency towards violence?"

"No," Bradan said. "I don't trust him. He could do anything."

"And he might not be alone," Olvina said.

Bradan's curiosity suddenly seemed to have picked up. So did Morley's.

"Why are you so certain about that?" Morley asked. Olvina immediately saw her mistake.

"We saw someone at the Dominion Day celebrations," Phoebe said.

"You saw someone suspicious and didn't tell us about him or her?" Bradan asked incredulously. "What did he look like?"

Olvina glanced at Phoebe. Both sisters looked ashamed.

"We were going to tell you about Uncle Nigel, but we got distracted," Olvina said.

"By your music and singing coming from the stage," Phoebe added.

"Did either of you see where he went?' Bradan asked.

Each sister shook her head.

Bradan didn't reply, but sat back in his chair. Olvina could see it irked Morley.

"Olvina, Phoebe, it is part of your duties to report any suspicious people, or goings on, to me. That's why you are here," Bradan said in a controlled, displeased tone. "We are short of trained police officers. This would not have slipped by if Ken and I were together. We tell each other everything we see."

"Sorry, sir," Phoebe said. "It won't happen again."

Slowly, anger drained from Bradan's face, but he looked like he knew something the rest didn't.

"Bradan, doesn't this disturb you just a little bit?" Morley said, guiding the conversation back to its former topic.

"I suppose it should bother me," Bradan said.

"But it doesn't," Morley said.

"I don't think Conrad will kill those girls like he threatened," Bradan said.

Morley said firmly, "I do."

"He insisted on getting Crystal," Olvina said.

"He's unsound," Phoebe said.

"All right, you've convinced me. Conrad is dangerous. But we are not calling Ken back from his vacation. I was left in charge. What do you think he'd do"

"He would thank you for calling him back," Olvina said, guessing.

This made Morley smile. Bradan turned his head and looked at her and then Phoebe.

"If he felt I couldn't handle the situation, he would demote me to the lowest Constable." After a pause to allow his words to sink in, he added, "What's Mr. Olson's role in this incident?"

Olvina's forehead furrowed in puzzlement. "That part remains a mystery to us. Mr. and Mrs. Olson were arguing and Mrs. Olson was in tears when I first peeked in their front window. Mr. Olson looked deeply upset about something."

"I don't believe for an instant Mr. Olson would become violent with his family," Uncle Bradan said. "There's got to be a third man involved."

Again Olvina noticed that I-know-something-you-might-not look they all hated crossed Bradan's face. Conrad's demands so far are, one, he wants his daughter back; two, three meals a day brought in; and three, a helicopter to get him safely out of the area once he has possession of Crystal."

"And you told him what?" Olvina asked.

"Crystal is not his daughter anymore," Phoebe said. "My dad and mom are her legal guardians. They adopted her. She is our sister."

"I made him know I wasn't to be intimidated and give into him. I didn't agree to any of his demands."

The radio on Bradan's shoulder sputtered, then Gerald's voice came through clear. "Dad, the SWAT team is here."

"We'll be right there," Bradan said.

Bradan stood. "Rest time is over."

"As Ken would say, 'So far, my friend, you've done a stellar job,'" Morley said.

Bradan smiled at Olvina and Phoebe, and reached out and set a friendly hand on each girl's shoulder. "With your help, of course."

***

As they prepared to leave the house, Morley handed Bradan a bulletproof jacket, which the veteran policeman put on before stepping outside.

At the chopper, Morley opened the door and Valiant leaped into the cab and rode with the human companions to the crime scene.

Chapter Six

Ten minutes later, Morley set the helicopter down on the green space between the two cabins, again keeping out of sight from those inside Olson's house.

Those gathered at the site were not surprised to see the helicopter arrive. All waited for them to come in that way, but not necessarily in the direction they came from. But right at the start, along with roadblocks, Bradan had posted a watch by the end of the driveway to keep a lookout for anyone or any vehicle approaching via the road. The approaching plane full of police officers, and two cadets, was spotted the instant it cleared the treetops north of them, not south, like they expected. But like Gay, all were well trained, and didn't raise murmurs loud enough to tip off the madman inside the house.

"Valiant, heel," Morley said to the dog. Valiant obeyed.

"I'm back," Bradan said to Murray, whom he had left in charge in his absence. Murray relinquished the telephone to his uncle. Before talking on the phone, Bradan paused. He turned and directed the SWAT team into position.

"All set, sir," one team member said to Bradan. "We have the suspect in my sights."

"Hold your fire."

"But, sir, I could take him out any second."

Bradan firmly repeated, "Hold your fire. Just because you have him in your sights doesn't mean shoot him."

Olvina and Phoebe exchanged smiles. It was just like the Ontario Provincial Police to settle a matter non-violently.

The officer curbed his eagerness immediately. "Yes, sir."

"And don't you ever forget that snipers are here only for backup," Bradan told the man.

Olvina and Phoebe looked on, their eagerness and willingness to assist the police growing, as the standoff progressed.

Bradan beamed a smile. "Now, Phoebe, Olvina, it's time for shift change. Morley will drive you two home."

"Who's taking our place? Uncle Bradan?" Phoebe asked.

"The usual. Kathleen, Lyle, and Cassia will pick up the slack," Bradan answered.

***

Exhausted from their hectic experiences, Olvina and Phoebe slept soundly when they went to bed that evening.

"You, Trevor and Kirk have a safe shift," Olvina said sleepily when Eunice left to fill her shift.

"Have a nice night," Phoebe said.

***

Olvina had slept well. The next morning she did feel a little tired and ached from getting up so early and all the activities strange to her.

Bradan turned towards the house and lifted the receiver to his lips. After setting the telephone on speakerphone his commanding voice boomed over the airwaves. His efficiency impressed Olvina. His movements were swift and fluid. His appearance, even, was commanding, yet as chief inspector there was still a humbleness about him.

"Conrad, come out onto the step and talk," he said.

The main door was open, the screen door in front of it closed.

Conrad moved close enough to the screen door to be exposed. He seemed to have been taken by surprise, like all the rest at the scene. "Is that you, Ken?"

"No. It's me."

"You again, Bradan? I didn't hear a helicopter."

"You must have been sleeping. Anyway, I'm back. Now what foolish trickery are you up to this time?"

"Isn't it obvious what I want? I want my daughter back. Did you bring Crystal? Where is she? I don't see her."

"You're not getting her back, not this way. She's not yours, she doesn't even bear your name anymore, and you're not even rightfully out of jail. You simply walked away from the work crew you were with. You're a fugitive, Conrad. Did you even stop to think how this would affect Crystal's life? Do you care? You will be back in a maximum-security prison when this is over. Think about this—Is all your pointless actions worth it all?"

"Like I told those ridiculously young kids assisting you, I'll kill these two babies in here if I don't get my daughter back."

Uncle Bradan glanced from Olvina to Phoebe. Olvina wondered if Uncle Conrad meant she and Phoebe were the ridiculously young ones, or if he meant Morley and the four recruits.

"The longer you take to decide, the more children will die."

Conrad's words sent cold chills up Olvina's spine, but Bradan said, composed, "I don't think even you will do that. Look around you, Conrad. There are SWAT team members positioned all around the house and on the rooftop. If anyone in that house dies, you die, too."

He paused and all silently waited for him to continue.

"It would be better for you if you surrendered right now."

"I'm not that stupid."

"It's up to you. We can wait you out. We can wait just as long as you can."

"We'll see about that." Conrad backed away from the doorway and slammed the inside door shut.

Olvina and Phoebe waited throughout the hot afternoon. Both girls were glad when evening came. The waiting continued. If it wasn't for obtaining permission from the cottage owner to use his house as a means for occasional rest, get a cool drink once in a while and get out of the hot sun, Olvina was certain they wouldn't have lasted very long.

At four in the afternoon, Cassia and Kathleen showed up to relieve Olvina and Phoebe so the two tired day cadets could go home. Yet every policeman remained on duty.

***

Midmorning the next day, Olvina joined Morley at the kitchen sink. There was no plumbing or electricity. Water was brought from the lake in a bucket. They drank from tall glasses.

Bradan suddenly turned to Olvina. "Didn't you tell me you saw Uncle Nigel.?"

"That's right. At the Dominion Day ceremonies."

"Which way did he go? Where did he go from there?"

"He hasn't been seen since. We don't know if he's hiding in the woods or not."

Bradan said, "And there's a train due through here in a short while."

Gerald said to his dad, "You're thinking exactly what I'm thinking."

"This man could be in these bushes lying in wait for the train and intending to hijack the entire unit as hostage," Olvina said.

"And Conrad seems the type as being unstable enough to start shooting at a trainload of passengers," Phoebe said.

"Either way, the passengers on the train are in grave danger," Bradan said.

He said to Morley softly, "You will have to get in contact with the engineer and see he goes on through without stopping, even if he does have a scheduled stop. I want you on this immediately and take as many officers as you think you need and do whatever it takes to accomplish what you have to. Bring the helicopter around. Go!"

"I'm on it already," Morley said.

Murray stepped up to Uncle Bradan. "I'll help."

"And me," Kirk offered.

"Count me in," Gerald said.

"Don't forget me," Lyle added.

"Thank you, all four of you," Bradan said, accepting their offer.

Olvina felt grateful right along with him.

Bradan said, "Now I'll need two female officers. Olvina, Phoebe, that's you two. We have a train loaded with passengers to get through here safely. Murray, you take a cruiser and drive out to the crossing by the highway, and from the crossing walk north for two miles. The train would clear Forest Lake at that mileage, and when it clears, give the all-clear signal. Take Phoebe with you. Get going. You have the furthest to go."

"We're on our way." Murray and Phoebe dashed for the cruiser.

Olvina waited for Bradan to give her instructions. She itched to do some real police work.

Bradan said to Kirk, "Follow the tracks on foot and look for objects on them that could stop, or even worse, derail a train. Gerald, you and Lyle beat the bushes along the track on both sides for a man hiding out. Hurry. We don't have much time. Olvina, you are just the person I need with me in the helicopter as a spotter."

Uncle Bradan, followed by Olvina, climbed aboard the helicopter. Morley, with Valiant lying on the floor by his seat, had already started the engine.

Olvina slid into the back seat, buckled in, while Uncle Bradan sat in the seat opposite Morley. Within seconds they were airborne and headed east out of Forest Lake.

Uncle Bradan talked on his phone to the train engineer.

Olvina had to listen closely to hear her uncle above the noise of the helicopter blades.

"This is Chief Inspector Turehue of the Forest Lake Police detachment. I'm trying to contact Train Sixty known to be traveling north on this line," he said.

"This is the engineer of Train Sixty."

"We have an explosive situation on the east side of Forest Lake."

"What is it and what do you want me to do?"

"There's a hostage situation and we don't want this train to stop, or even so much as slow down, on its way through. We will meet you by helicopter and escort you through Forest Lake and six miles beyond to make sure the tracks are clear. Once you get the all clear from us, keep the train moving until you reach your destination up by James Bay. I'm notifying police departments all along the route to make sure you don't stop for anything. The police at your destination will make sure passengers slated to get off between get home. Do you understand me?"

"Yes, sir."

"Are the conductors handy?"

"Yes, they're in the cab with me."

"They can make sure every passenger stays down and away from the windows. And keep those whistles silent while approaching any town between here and Timmins. Do you read me?"

"Yes, sir. We can't be any more than twenty minutes out of Forest Lake now. Right on schedule, too. We'll be there at three o'clock P.M. sharp."

Bradan ended the call, then said, "Now we wait and see what happens next."

Below, Olvina saw Gerald walking beside his younger brother. The two were beating every inch of the trees growing alongside the railroad track. Progress proved faster close to the railroad crossing as not much brush grew there, but the further east they went the woods grew thicker along with the underbrush.

Those on the ground were bathed in the sun's unwelcome warmth, nearly everyone wiping sweat away from their eyes and foreheads.

Kirk's voice came over the chopper radio. "There's Blanche River. And the south end of Lake Forest."

Olvina watched as the men arrived at the bridge and started across.

Kirk wiped sweat from his eyes with the back of his hand. "Would I love to dive into that water and cool off."

Bradan heard the comment via his phone and said, "You'd better not. We should be meeting the train any minute."

The helicopter rounded a gentle curve.

Olvina pointed along the tracks ahead of them. "There's Train Sixty."

The long line of passenger cars had come into view, just little dots in the distance. Morley easily lifted the helicopter higher just in time to miss the dome in the lead diesel engine.

The aircraft put the police on the same level as the train cab so Bradan didn't have any trouble seeing the engineer or the engineer couldn't miss seeing him.

He waved him on through. "And remember, keep those whistles silent as you approach Forest Lake."

"I will, sir."

Bradan turned to Morley. "Now we escort him through, all the way to where Murray and Phoebe are waiting."

The train approached the crossing by Golden Ridge. The two leading diesel engines and coaches went by.

Olvina watched until the entire line of cars had passed by and out of sight.

"I've never seen an object as huge as a train move so silently," she said. This brought smiles to the lips of Bradan and Morley.

A few minutes later, Bradan called Murray.

"All's clear at this end," Murray said.

"The train is out of sight of the town limits of Forest Lake," Phoebe said.

"Excellent. Mission accomplished," Bradan said. "Murray, Phoebe, return to Forest Lake. You can help look for the third man."

"The mysterious third man?" Murray questioned. "That maniac that's hiding out in the bushes?"

"I don't think he's so mysterious," Olvina said.

"Or a maniac," Phoebe said.

Morley petted the silky fur on Valiant's neck.

"If there's anyone there we'll flush him out."

Chapter Seven

Bradan ended the call, but left the phone on for emergencies. He turned his gaze to look at the girls. "Olvina, Phoebe, get some sleep now. Be back here tomorrow at oh-eight-hundred."

"What time is that?" Phoebe asked

"Eight o'clock in the morning," Olvina said.

***

The next morning, Olvina awoke early. Phoebe slept peacefully in the other bed. Still wearing her pajamas, Olvina leaped to the floor and started dressing. Phoebe slept on. She looked so content under the covers in the chill of the early morning that Olvina envied her. She'd hate to disturb her, but knew she had to.

Olvina gently shook her sister. Phoebe muttered something she didn't understand.

"Time to get up for breakfast, then back to helping Uncle Bradan," Olvina said.

Phoebe pushed back the covers and leaned on her elbows. She rubbed sleepy eyes with one hand.

"I now question the wisdom of being a police cadet and helping Uncle Bradan," Phoebe grumbled.

Olvina smiled. "Just think, people like Uncle Conrad have to be stopped."

"Let the police do it," Phoebe said.

Olvina laughed and pulled the covers off her. "Hurry."

Dressed in her nightgown, Phoebe got out of bed and started dressing. She was brushing her teeth when Olvina finished pulling on her socks and started towards the bathroom. Phoebe turned on the shower as Olvina went downstairs.

Later, after breakfast, Olvina, then Phoebe, hugged the rest of the family good-bye for the day.

"I'll see you after four o'clock," Martin called after them as they went out the door.

The girls were at the bottom of Golden Ridge.

"Let's go this way," Phoebe said. "Let's cut through the yard of McCall's cottage."

"But it isn't even on the path to Olson's," Olvina said. "I doubt if we will get there any sooner."

But Phoebe didn't seem to hear and kept going her own way. Olvina hesitated only a second then followed.

The girls came to an old building.

"This building once housed livestock," Phoebe said.

"I don't remember any being kept here since we came to live with Mom and Dad," Olvina said. "The windows are filthy. I can't even see through them."

She stopped to peer through a window. She drew back.

"This is weird."

"And scary," Phoebe added.

Curious, Olvina peeked into the interior gloom, through the doorless opening. She heard a noise and an eerie feeling gripped her. Shaking it off, she told herself mice, squirrels, and stray cats would love to live in an abandoned building like this. Quickly, she withdrew and started along a path towards the railroad tracks...in the opposite direction she should be going.

"Why is this path so well packed?" she asked.

"Could be trails made by wild wolves and the like looking for food," Phoebe said.

Olvina looked over her shoulder.

"What's that shape standing almost hidden in the doorway?" She gasped. "I don't remember anything being there when I peeked in."

Phoebe started running.

Olvina followed.

Soon, in the distance she saw officers working hard to get through an extraordinarily rocky area with a thick patch of trees. Olvina turned and looked behind her. A form on the tracks caught her eye. She continued running as fast as she could, Phoebe right beside her, along the railroad ties between the tracks towards their cousins.

"We see someone," she said to Gerald. The sound of the helicopter blades chopping the air rose in her ears, then a second or two later, the craft came into view.

"What do they see?" Bradan asked.

"Just saw a form," Olvina said.

"Was it the shape of a man or beast?' Bradan asked.

"I'm sure it was a man," Phoebe answered.

"Where?" inquired Bradan.

"Behind Phoebe and me in the bush alongside the tracks about half a mile."

"Why are you there?" Bradan asked from the air.

Olvina noticed Phoebe blush

"I guess we got sidetracked," Phoebe said.

"Eunice and Trevor have gone home already for a much needed rest. Lucky for you two, I'm short of help here," Uncle Bradan said.

"You are back at the cabins?" Olvina asked.

"No. I'm with Morley in the helicopter," Bradan answered. "Murray and Lyle are watching the Olson place."

Phoebe ventured a look the way they'd come, but saw no one. "He must have gone into the bush on the other side."

"He did, and I didn't get a good look at him," Bradan said.

"Bradan, that third man you mentioned. It...is it? Naw, it couldn't be. It's impossible," Morley said.

Bradan said, laughter in his voice, "I see you have it all figured out. Yes, it could be and it is."

"How could have I been so stupid so as not to think of him before this?"

Morley sounded so distraught the girls felt sorry for him.

"You aren't stupid," Bradan said. "You've been preoccupied fighting a war here. Conrad didn't give you much opportunity to think of anything else. At least you did figure it out. We'll have to cut him off before he gets into Olson's."

Morley swung the helicopter towards the corduroy road leading to the meadow surrounding Olson's house.

Below, Olvina and Phoebe followed the officers. They hurried down the track embankment. They ran across a grassy meadow between the tracks and narrow band of birch trees, pine, and small willows next to the meadow where Olson's lived.

Olvina tried to cut the runaway off. Instead, he headed for the jungle of trees and undergrowth alongside the road.

Morley flew the chopper over the area. Three times they rooted the fugitive out of his hiding place. Phoebe saw him dash across an open spot. He disappeared into another patch of thick undergrowth.

Morley circled the area with ever-decreasing-sized circles until the man was trapped in one small corner. The helicopter hovered over the ground searchers.

"We saw him in there several times," Kirk said into his radio microphone. "The woods are thick and we've lost him. But we're certain he's holed up in a small area. We're positive he's in there."

"All right," Bradan said.

Those on the ground heard him say to Morley, "We will have to land and search on foot. Over and out."

Morley landed the chopper and everyone, including Valiant, scrambled off.

The excitement of the chase thrilled Olvina. One glance at Phoebe made her wonder if her sister felt the same way. Her face looked pale and she appeared tired, but Phoebe bravely said to the fully-trained police officers, "He won't get very far in there. Beyond this narrow strip of solid ground stretches endless miles of bottomless bog called muskeg. The area is known as Tamarack Marsh."

"I wonder if he knows that?" Gerald said.

Bradan said, "I think he does. He's likely hoping we won't remember. He wants us to go in there and get ourselves hopelessly bogged down long enough for him to make good on his escape."

"Where did he go from here?" Murray asked.

"Before we make another move, we need to ask for God's guidance," Bradan said. "Let's all join hands and pray."

When they had formed a circle, heads bowed and eyes closed, Bradan began, "I ask You that this standoff will soon come to a peaceful settlement and we will be able to flush out Mr. Weistien as we all are sure that's who it is. Amen."

"We will thoroughly pound every inch of woods back to the track and to where we were before," Bradan said.

"I have a better idea," announced Morley.

"Are you going to send Valiant in?" Olvina asked.

"Go ahead," Uncle Bradan said when Morley nodded.

Morley, with Valiant on a twenty-foot leather leash attached to a leather harness, led the officers through the thick jungle.

Olvina and Phoebe remained behind the group. The girls had to dodge trees, jump over fallen ones, and climb over uprooted tree roots in order to keep up.

Morley came to a halt; Bradan stopped beside him. Olvina stood beside Bradan with Phoebe on Morley's left side.

"The man came this way," Morley said.

Olvina turned her gaze downward. Phoebe followed her direction.

"There is a trail of broken twigs and bent-over grass," Phoebe said.

"Where did he go from here?" Bradan said. "Can either of you girls tell me?"

Olvina shook her head.

Phoebe said, "No, I can't."

Bradan turned to the rookies. "Search the ground for footprints. Search those outbuildings for anything that could be used to stop a train."

Bradan gazed in the direction the prints led, and looked straight at the old little barn on the edge of the property sandwiched between the tracks and Uncle Eric's property, the same place the girls had just passed on their way to the tracks. The two houses stood only yards apart, but the little barn was a ways from the main house.

Valiant had other ideas. He strained at the end of his leash. Olvina could tell his heart was set to go in a direction not one of the policemen thought of looking.

"Anyone living there right now?" Bradan asked.

"No," Olvina said.

She was about to say more, but Bradan cut in. "I know. The father,

Mr. Eugene McKay, used to live here full time but then his dad got a job south, so they moved. Gene McKay is a friend of mine and Uncle Ken's. He brings his family here for summer vacations, as well as other holidays."

Uncle Bradan turned and looked at Morley. "Let Valiant do what he has to do."

"Look at this," Morley said. "Valiant thinks we should go there."

Bradan looked in the direction Valiant pointed his nose. He held up an arm to shield his eyes against the sunlight glinting off the shimmering blue waters of Wan Asquinn. Bradan looked back at the house and barn.

"Why not let Valiant loose?" Phoebe said.

"Let him decide which is the best way to go," Olvina said.

Bradan nodded. Morley undid the snap attached to a ring on the Shilo Shepherd's harness. "Find."

Valiant sprang forward in the direction of the waters of the bay.

"Olvina, Phoebe, stay behind me," Bradan said and started after Morley and his dog. The girls followed.

In seconds, he and Morley stopped on the sandy shores of the bay. Only a few yards away Olvina saw Trevor, Wapinkino, and Lorne Prestone at the docks. Lorne Prestone lived in Lakeview but attended Golden Ridge Baptist School. During the school year he boarded with Martin and his family. During summer vacation he spent a lot of time with Trevor.

Lorne and Wapinkino leaned against the bow of the boat, waiting, Trevor's attention riveted on gassing up the boat's eighty-horse-power engine. He held the gas pump to the gas tank and squeezed the trigger to let the gas flow.

Olvina turned her gaze to what was happening out in the bay. She could see Valiant had caught up with Nigel. The two of them stopped in the water face-to-face. Nigel stood in the water up to his knees, Valiant up to his furry belly.

Olvina shivered when she saw Nigel had a pistol in one hand, pointed right at the dog's head.

Phoebe saw it, too. Each girl released her breath through tight lips, glad when this didn't intimidate the valiant dog.

Valiant reared, fangs bared, and bravely faced his enemy as he had been trained to do. He went for the gun arm. The gun slid from Nigel's grasp. It hit the water with a loud plop. The pistol sank out of sight.

Olvina knew the gun would be useless now, but Nigel got down on his knees and searched anyway. He located the firearm. He picked it up and heaved it as far as he could into deeper water, then started swimming.

"He's going to try and swim to that point across the bay," Gerald said.

Olvina had other ideas. "He's luring poor Valiant out to deeper water. That man must be desperate to escape."

"More like desperate not to be seen. I can't understand why," Phoebe said.

"He doesn't want Sihon or Crystal to see him," Olvina said.

Chapter Eight

By now Bradan recognized the man in the water. "I think that fool has it in mind to drown that animal."

Man and dog were way out in the middle of the bay. Uncle Nigel kept swimming and so did Valiant, but the dog knew enough to stay far away from the man so he couldn't grasp him and push him underwater.

Morley said, "Valiant is a strong swimmer, sir. It won't be him that drowns. I've trained him in twelve-mile endurance running beside me on horseback, swimming behind rowboats and in every kind of situation he would encounter."

Meanwhile, the suspect worked his way out into deeper water. Valiant followed, determined.

Nigel headed directly for the point of land. Valiant followed.

"Our friend is tiring," Bradan said.

Olvina said, "You do know who he is?"

Uncle Bradan remained tight-lipped and silent.

Out of the corner of her eye, on the dock, Olvina saw Trevor release the trigger, pull back the pump and set it down. The gas tank on the boat motor was full.

"We sure do," Bradan said softly, at last. That was all he said on the subject. "Come on, we can't just stand here. We'll have to be over there on that point of land when he gets there."

"I'll take Gerald and Kirk with me and meet the suspect on the other side," Morley said.

"You do that," agreed Bradan. "Murray and Lyle will keep an eye on Conrad. Olvina and Phoebe come with me in the boat."

Bradan started towards the docks. Trevor, Lorne, and Wapinkino were already in the craft, and had moved away from the dock. Trevor had the motor tipped in the water, preparing to start the engine to set off on their adventure.

"Stop!" Bradan called.

But no one in the boat heard him over the noise of Trevor pulling on the cord to start the engine.

"Stop!" Bradan called, louder. He had to shout once more.

The third time, Wapinkino heard and looked back towards the dock.

Bradan waved his arms. Wapinkino touched Lorne's shoulder with one hand, and spoke to Trevor. At that moment, the motor chose to start.

Trevor turned the boat in a slow circle and headed back to the dock.

"We need that craft for police work," Bradan said.

"But Mr. Turehue," Wapinkino said, "we were about to enjoy a couple of hours on the lake fishing."

Bradan didn't relent. "We need the boat."

The boys stepped aside and Bradan and his companions leaped aboard.

Trevor hadn't shut off the motor.

"Get us over there," Olvina said, pointing towards where Valiant and his victim still quarreled over who would reach land first.

Bradan added, "Please, be swift about it!"

"They've almost reached the point of land," Phoebe said.

Trevor turned the boat towards the point. Soon they skimmed over the waves. In seconds he slowed the craft beside the swimmers.

"It's at this point the shallow waters of the bay drop suddenly to the real deep waters Lake Forest," Olvina shouted above the noise of the motor.

A wind from the northwest blew down the length of the lake and swept around the point of land. Waves crashed against the rocky shore, curled back upon themselves, and caused treacherous undercurrents

Morley, Gerald, and Kirk came into view on the point a few minutes later.

Bradan said, "We have him now. You can call off your dog."

"Valiant, come," Morley said.

Olvina admired how obediently the dog veered away from his victim and swam for shore. He tried pulling himself out of the water, but the waves were strong and the rocks slippery.

Olvina glanced at her sister.

"His claws can't find traction on the slippery rocks," Phoebe said.

The brave animal fell back into the troubled waves.

Feeling helpless, Olvina exchanged looks with Trevor. The look on his face told her he hated himself for being unable to help the dog. The five teens all sat in the boat, unable to do a thing.

"Valiant isn't going to drown, is he?" Lorne said.

Morley moved closer to the waterline and waited for his dog to try climbing out again. When Valiant did, Morley reached down and grabbed the dog by the harness and helped him onto a grassy knoll on the rocks away from the wind and waves. Olvina breathed a sigh of relief, along with her friends.

Trevor skillfully maneuvered the boat close to the rocks where the waves were less treacherous.

Bradan scrambled out, joining his colleagues on the rocky shore. Bradan turned to Trevor. "Wait here." His gaze left his nephew and went from Olvina to Lorne to Wapinkino. "And don't get out of this boat."

"How's your dog?" Bradan asked Morley, once he was on shore.

"He's fine. That swim didn't even tire him."

Those in the boat could see the waves had carried the suspect closer to the rocks in this sheltered area, so it was easier for him to pull himself out of the water and start climbing higher to get above his pursuers.

Morley proved quicker.

"Attack!" his voice rang out.

In one swift, efficient motion, Valiant closed the distance, grabbed Nigel as the man was about to start climbing, and in one unruffled movement got his pant leg and dragged him down off the plateau he had managed to gain.

Olvina's pulse raced as Kirk moved in and quickly had the criminal's hands pinned behind his back. Cousin Gerald was there to assist with the handcuffing. Olvina hoped Kirk knew how to handle his weapon as he stood ready with a pistol raised.

"Don't shoot, Bradan," those in the boat heard Nigel plead.

Olvina sighed. Trevor sighed. Phoebe sighed. Wapinkino sighed, and Lorne sighed when, in an instant, the suspect was on his knees on leaves and moss, subdued. Kirk lowered his pistol and re-holstered.

Unable to remain still any longer, Olvina leaped the short distance from the boat onto the rocks, and with the others streaming behind her, ran as fast as she could over the uneven ground to join the policemen. Wapinkino remained behind, paddle in hand to keep the wind and waves from pounding the boat against the rocks.

Nigel spoke up bravely. "Bradan, I don't mean anyone any harm. The men inside that house are the ones you have to watch. They're both crazy."

"Don't believe this man for one second when he says he doesn't mean us any harm," Bradan said.

"It is you," Olvina said.

"Uncle Nigel," Phoebe said.

Olvina shook her head in disbelief. Her mind went back to Morley's house the previous evening and understood why Bradan had acted as if he knew something the rest of the unit didn't and had taken this all so calmly.

"Get him in the boat and take us back to the dock," Bradan said.

"Wapinkino and I will wait right here for you to come back and then we'll go out on the lake," Lorne said.

"Good idea," Bradan said.

Wapinkino and Lorne moved away from the boat and found a grassy ridge to sit and wait.

Kirk and Gerald escorted their prisoner back to the boat.

"I'm truly going to recommend a police dog training academy in this department," Bradan said to Morley with a smile. "Valiant has certainly proved with flying colors he has what it takes to be a police dog, and you certainly have the talent to train the dogs. Starting the unit will be given top priority and will go through immediately. You, will head this unit. I know you've waited a long time for this."

The rest all heard what Bradan said.

Lyle looked at Morley with a huge smile. "Congratulations."

"What will you call the kennel?" Olvina asked.

"I think L'Valiant Police Dog Academy," Morley said.

"I like the name," Phoebe said.

"Classy," Trevor said.

"That's nice," Olvina agreed.

"Sounds nice," Wapinkino added.

After helping their prisoner aboard, Kirk, Gerald and Bradan got on the boat as well.

"Take us back to the dock," Bradan said to his nephew.

Olvina rode back to the dock in complete silence. She wondered, We have one man in custody. How long would take us to take Uncle Conrad in?

Once all were safely on the dock, Braden said to the boaters, "We appreciate your cooperation."

"My pleasure, Uncle Bradan," Trevor said. "We were delighted to assist."

"Gerald, Murray, you two search that old barn," Bradan said to his nephews.

Once they started searching the dilapidated barn, it didn't take Kirk and Gerald long to let Bradan know about the objects they found.

"We found bright-colored flags that the engineer would see at a distance and would be able to bring the train to a halt right where you stood," Gerald reported.

Bradan looked straight at the prisoner, his brown eyes steadily holding the other's gaze.

"Brilliant!" Bradan said. "You and your half-brother, Conrad, planned to stop that train and hold everyone on it as hostage until Conrad's demands were met."

"Especially the one concerning getting his daughter back,' Nigel said. "But, I'm not in the planning."

Olvina listened to all this in disbelief. Her knees felt weak. "You're Sihon's father, aren't you?"

"You guessed it."

"And Phoebe and I walked right by that stupid barn and you were inside?"

"That's right."

"Why did you follow us?"

"Why do you think?"

"So you could add us to your list of hostages."

"No. It's not my list."

"And I didn't even realize what danger we were in."

"You are in no danger from me. My so-called brother is crazy. Maybe he has been all along. I just wouldn't see it."

"Is Conrad on drugs or anything like that?" Phoebe asked.

"I think so. He's the devil himself."

"Never mind, don't say anymore," Bradan cautioned gently. "Come with us. We can take the shortcut across the field. Conrad is not the devil but he is indwelt, therefore controlled by the devil. Consider yourself safe here with us."

Kirk stepped out of the shelter of the woods as the group tried to cross the meadow into the yard by the cottages.

"I heard a shot," he said.

Bradan answered, shaken in spite of his being a veteran cop, "A bullet whipped past my ear."

"Another shot," Olvina said. "A heavy rifle this time."

"Does anyone know where the bullet landed?" Phoebe said.

"I heard the thud as the bullet entered the packed sand and rock of the embankment on the other side of the track," Olvina said. "The bullet followed a path that would have traveled right through the window of a train coach."

"Another shot," Bradan cried. "Get back."

Quickly, the girls followed as policemen scrambled for cover.

"He tried to shoot me," the prisoner exclaimed in disbelief.

"We'll never get back that way," Gerald.

"We'll have to go the long way around," Bradan said.

Kirk looked doubtful. "What if he sees us going the long way around?"

"That is possible," Gerald said.

Kirk waved his hand towards the railroad crossing. "There is an open area by the crossing and the first two houses."

Bradan looked across the field. He could easily see Olson's house since it was mere yards away. He looked at the upstairs window.

"Listen up, now. The shot came from Olson's. That roof is way higher than the rest of the roofs around it."

"Agreed. This height would give Uncle Conrad a clear view of what went on by the tracks, and also give him a clear shot. But, Uncle Bradan, are you right in assuming Uncle Conrad would not shoot again?" Olvina said.

"You tell me," Bradan said.

"It's the prisoner he wants in his sights, and if he doesn't see him, then what will he do?" Phoebe said.

Chapter Nine

Nigel said, "He won't shoot at anyone but me."

"We'll need a decoy," Olvina said.

"We'll need some officers to walk across the field and draw his attention away from us," Phoebe said.

Olvina looked around the group. Not one so much as blinked an eye, afraid that even something so small might be taken as a bid to volunteer.

Bradan asked when Olvina thought they'd been kept waiting long enough, "Any volunteers?" Bradan looked at his son, then Kirk. He said brightly, "Didn't I once hear one or two of you say how much you were eager to sink your teeth into some real police work? Here's your chance. Get going. The rest of us will meet you in the police circle."

There were mumbled "Yes, sirs."

Gerald and Kirk started towards the open field.

"Come on," Gerald said. His cousin followed without question. Kirk and Gerald made their way through the long grass, ducking behind the tall weeds or some low growing trees to remain out of sight.

Bradan, his captive, Morley, Olvina and Phoebe started the trek by a different way back to base.

When Olvina and Phoebe arrived at the command post, Bradan stood beside Murray and Lyle, watching the three cross the field. Bradan nodded in approval. Gerald and Kirk dove into a tall patch of green grass and waited a few seconds to see if any shots would be fired. When nothing happened, Gerald led his brother and cousin towards the command post. This time they made it.

Olvina took a section of the tape in one hand while Phoebe grabbed another part. Together, they lifted the tape so the youths could easily step over.

"Welcome back," Bradan said. He turned to Nigel,

"Come with me and give us your statement." Bradan guided him to a less crowded spot where chairs and a table had been set in the cabin's shade.

"How is that incident turning out?" Murray asked. "Anyone injured?" Lyle said

"None so far," Uncle Bradan said.

Nigel said to Bradan, "I'd like to know your reasoning for sending those youngsters into such a dangerous adventure."

"There was no real danger," Uncle Bradan responded. "I reasoned that Conrad meant that shot for you. The shot came the instant you and I stepped out into the field, and I didn't think he would shoot until he saw you again."

"And he didn't," Nigel said.

"He wanted to warn you he wasn't happy about something and not to betray him," Bradan said.

Nigel's manner was not arrogant; instead, it held more like awe, a lifetime of repressed admiration, released at that moment. "You again, Bradan." He looked straight at him; again his tone holding nothing but respect. "You, the highly decorated Chief Inspector, hero of many life-and-death situations. You've come a long way since we were boys, Bradan Gerald Turehue." His eyes grew distant before he spoke again. "And your partner, Kenneth Murray Asquinn, Chief Superintendent and also highly decorated, and hero of many a standoff. What happened to the days when you were known as plain 'Kenny and Bradan' and whatever Conrad and I were called when we were boys?"

"We're still known as 'Ken' or 'Bradan' to a lot of people—most of them are our friends," Bradan said. "You've never regarded us as just plain 'Ken' or 'Bradan,' nor have we ever been friends."

"Oh, but I remember we were at one time. At least Ken's brother, Marty, and his twin sister, Martha, and I were. We were the same age. I remember the short time I lived with his family when my own family didn't want me. Those few months have stayed with me all this time."

There was silence as Bradan and Nigil thought back to those days long ago. The story went, the way Olvina and Phoebe heard it, Nigel had lived with the Asquinns for a short while. During that short stay God's Holy Spirit had convicted the boy he was a sinner, and gently drew him to God's way of salvation. There, in the small but adequate bedroom Nigel had bowed to God's plan for his life. Then one day Conrad had lured the boy back home and since then, the girls doubted, Nigel had heard the word of God once.

Olvina felt a kinship with this poor wretched and abused lad.

"How did you and Conrad end up together here in Forest Lake?" Bradan asked. "I know you were not released from jail. You weren't in jail. Your brother escaped."

Nigel shrugged. "I suddenly felt the strong urge to come to Forest Lake. I couldn't resist it. I immediately set out for here. Conrad and I were to have met in front of that place where the ceremonies were. But then I remembered how to resist his long-distance controlling. I resisted and he hasn't bothered me since. "

"Conrad knows how to control from a distance," Bradan said. "More of his voodoo."

"Those involved in witchcraft use those dolls," Olvina said. "He would stick pins in the doll, which in his mind, would be you. He would say something like," she changed her voice to sound like a devil-worshiping high priest chanting, "Nigel Weistien, this is the master speaking. Meet me in Forest Lake."

Nigil looked at the teens with awe. He knew this is exactly what went on.

Bradan said, "Sorry, Nigel, we are not ready to accept your explanation."

A shocked look passed over Phoebe's face. She glanced at Olvina.

"What isn't there to believe?" Nigel said. To Olvina and Phoebe he sounded to be begging to be believed.

"I believe you worked right along with your half-brother to try and get Crystal back, but the police surrounding the house cut off any means of you returning to the place and communicating with Conrad."

Nigel shook his head. "Conrad is on his own in this. He should be wearing down soon. I resisted his voodoo, but I did come to make sure he didn't harm my son or niece."

Olvina noticed how tenderly Nigel spoke of Sihon, his son. His face transformed into soft lines.

"I believe you," Bradan assured the distraught young man.

"How is my son?"

"Sihon is fine," he replied.

"And my niece?"

"Crystal and Sihon are both fine."

"Can I see Sihon?"

"Not right away. When this is over with."

"Uncle Bradan, a man is climbing out a top floor window and is headed this way," Murray said.

Bradan immediately sprang to his feet. "Can you see who it is?'

"No, we can't. Wait, it's Wapinkino."

Wapinkino let himself down to the ground from the kitchen roof and joined them.

Olvina noticed he looked scruffy and dirty, his hair stuck out in every direction, his clothes messed up. But then, she thought to herself, no one that had been in this incident from the start did look all that neat and tidy.

"How did you escape?" Bradan asked.

Wapinkino pointed towards a window on the east end of the upstairs. "I climbed out that window onto the kitchen roof and slid safely to the ground."

"What's your father's role in that house?"

"At first he wasn't nice to any of the family. Dad and I had words, Mom and Dad had words, and he even made Mom cry, then as this incident went on and on, he had a change of attitude and seemed genuinely concerned about our safety."

"What does Mr. Cameron have for weapons?"

"My dad's entire gun collection. A twenty-two, pellet guns, hunting rifles, as well as an old British army rifle. But Dad had them stored properly in gun cabinets, locked, and the ammunition in another compartment in another part of the house. Mr. Cameron had to break the glass front of the gun cabinet to gain use of the weapons, and break the ammunition drawer lock to get the bullets."

"We'll take into consideration what he just told us, Wapinkino," Bradan said. To Morley, he said,. "Take Nigel down to the station and lock him up for his own safety."

"Hello," a voice called from behind them.

Startled, Olvina jumped.

"That sounds like Mom," Phoebe said.

Everyone turned to see who had spoken.

Martin and his twin stood right behind them.

"We thought you would all be hungry by now," Martin said.

"A bunch of us put together a few sandwiches and brought them to you," Martha said.

"We brought cold, fresh water from the store, too," Martin said.

"Thank you, Martin, Martha. It's getting more and more difficult to sit still in this heat," Morley said. He wiped sweat from his brow with the back of his hand.

"I wonder how much longer this will go on?" Martin asked.

"I feel apprehensive about the safety of those children and Mrs. Olson," Martha said.

Olvina was uneasy. "Me too, Mom."

"It's scary, them still in the same house as that gunman," Phoebe said.

"I wish we could do something, Martin said.

"I feel so helpless," Martha said.

"It's best you leave the sandwiches and drinks there on the step and get back to safety," Bradan said. "Thank you. Thank the rest for us."

The twins set down the boxes, turned around and left the way they had arrived. Soon they disappeared from sight around the corner of the first cottage.

Bradan opened the box of sandwiches and the food was passed out.

Bottles of water were handed out as well.

"Prayer always helps. We could ask God that this episode will soon be over with, peacefully," Phoebe added.

Both the veteran and less experienced cops fell silent. Lips moved in silent prayer as they prayed God would keep the girls safe, and for the safety of the rest of the hostages as well as the police officers on site, to bring this criminal—or criminals—to justice.

The prayer over, Bradan said, "There must be a way to get in contact with those kids. I would feel a lot better if those children were safe somewhere else."

"We can circle the house and see if there's a way," Olvina said.

Bradan turned to Morley. "Take Olvina, Murray and Lyle with you. Phoebe, you stay with me."

"What shall I look for?"

"Look for an open downstairs bedroom." In spite of the heat, Morley appeared ready for action immediately.

"Come on, Murray, Lyle, and Olvina." He started across the yard, trailed by the two young policemen, and Olvina. He kept his phone on so he could keep Bradan constantly informed as to what was happening.

At the front of the house, Olvina paused. "It's the master bedroom. I see some of the younger children on the bed, but can't make out which ones."

Morley repeated this information to the rest over the radio. "I frown on him for not thinking to leave the window open more than half way."

Although they talked in whispers, the noise alerted the children huddled together on the bed. But those Olvina could see through the window were well known to them; they knew they were policemen and wouldn't hurt any of them so settled down.

Bradan spoke over the two-way radio. "Go ahead and climb in and hand those children out to us. This couldn't turn out better."

Morley smiled at Olvina. "Just the job we need people like you for. You are slim enough to slip in under a half-closed window."

"I see the two youngest girls in the room and it was them I was most worried about."

"Go. Someone will follow once you open the window wider."

Olvina pushed herself up onto the window ledge, and then climbed silently the rest of the way into the room. On light feet she crept over to the bed, all the while holding her fingers to her lips, indicating to the children to remain silent.

"Hand out the two youngest girls. Those two babies are in the most danger," Bradan instructed over the radio. Olvina heard him speaking to someone back at the post, "Kirk, you stand by and be ready to take them from Ger, and then hand them back to me and I will hand them to Phoebe. Ready, Olvina?"

"Yes," Olvina murmured.

She picked up Eileen, who had been nestled in the arms of an older brother. She was the only fair-haired toddler of the family, taking after her father, who was Norwegian by nationality. All the rest of the children were dark like their Metis mother.

Then she picked up Susan. Olvina started towards the window where Murray waited.

Once these two were safe, Olvina went back to the bed. Bobby let out a loud cry. Swiftly, Olvina picked up Bobby in her arms. "Come on, Nadine," she said to the oldest sister, who was old enough to look after herself, and dashed for the window. She handed Bobby to Murray, who passed them along. Phoebe stepped up to Morley and took her in her arms. She carried her to Wapinkino. Wapinkino took his sister into the safety of his arms.

Olvina reached for Nadine and picked her up for Murray to take, when the bedroom doorknob turned. She stopped in her tracks, glanced back at her cousin and whispered, "Some one's coming."

"I know," whispered Murray.

The door opened and all movement stopped. Mrs. Olson stood in the doorway. She was alone.

"What's wrong?" Bradan asked.

"I'm not sure," Morley said and repeated the question to his cousin.

"Mrs. Olson has come into the room," Olvina whispered, and the message was passed along.

"What's wrong? I heard Bobby cry," Mrs. Olson asked, and then caught sight of Olvina and Murray by the window.

She immediately grasped what was going on, and said in a loud voice, "Everything's under control here. I'll leave you guys to get some rest."

Backing out of the room, Mrs. Olson closed the door. Murray helped Olvina climb out and jump to the ground, then they all made an escape back to the cordoned-off area.

Olvina smiled at her sister, Phoebe smiled back. Both hearts danced with joy when they saw the children were all secure in the embrace of their oldest brother, Snow Owl.

Bradan said, "To use Ken's words, 'stellar work.'

"Knowing these children are safe is a big relief to both Phoebe and me," Olvina said.

"It was nothing," Phoebe said as if they had just finished shoveling snow off the house roof in the wintertime, or some other miscellaneous chore.

"Is everyone out?" inquired Bradan.

"No, sir," Wapinkino said.

Chapter Ten

"There are three more—Aires, Mom and Dad," Wapinkino said.

"Where is Aires?" Olvina inquired. "I didn't see anything of him."

"Me and Aires were in an upstairs bedroom. After I returned home, we were all in the front room for a while, me, Dad, and Mom. Mom and Dad quarreled fiercely at first. Mr. Cameron seemed to enjoy that. Dad got friendlier with Mom, and I'm sure Mom and Dad are ready to get back together. I was the only one able to escape before that madman came and stopped me."

"Do you want us to go after Aires?" Olvina said.

"No, it's too risky," Bradan said. "Besides, I don't think it will be necessary. Our man in there will surrender soon, especially when he finds out he doesn't have those two babies as leverage anymore. We'll wait him out. We've delayed this long, so a little more time won't hurt us. I can't see this siege going on much longer. Conrad will likely surrender peacefully."

He looked around at the spots where the SWAT team had been positioned. "They're ready for anything," he said, with satisfaction.

Kathleen and Cassia joined them.

"Cadets Kathleen and Cassia Asquinn reporting for the four o'clock shift," Kathleen said to Bradan.

Bradan turned to the day cadets. "Olvina, Phoebe, you may go home now."

Olvina and Phoebe rushed home. Phoebe was the first to shower and change from her sweaty cadet uniform into fresh, clean clothes. Olvina, after clean up as well, met her sister, Lorne, and Wapinkino outside in the little patch of Martin's front lawn. Eunice slept in the quint's room, resting for the night shift at midnight. Trevor slept on Sihon's bed. Sihon and Crystal remained close to their adoptive parents, Martin and Audrey Asquinn.

There was absolutely nothing to do. To add to this boredom, the sun blazed down from a cloudless sky into Martin's yard and there was hardly any shade.

"We should be able to go down to the docks," Sihon said.

That was all the urging Olvina needed. "Come on. Let's go." She was on her feet sneaking through the hedge, then running along the trail to the tracks in a flash.

Sihon started to follow, but Martin's voice stopped him. "Sihon!"

Sihon skidded to a halt on the gravely road.

"You can't go, neither can Crystal. Uncle Bradan said to keep a close eye on you two."

"Aw, Dad. I'm sick of sitting around the yard."

"Come on back," Martin said.

Sihon turned and walked slowly back to the yard.

***

Upon reaching the tracks, Olvina stopped short, a millisecond ahead of Phoebe, then, Lorne and Wapinkino.

"Uncle Bradan, Kathleen, and Morley are at the dock," Olvina said.

"Maybe we shouldn't go down there," Lorne said.

"Why not? Why are you suddenly afraid of Uncle Bradan and our sister?"

"Mr. Turehue did tell everyone to remain close to home and out of danger," Wapinkino said.

"We are close to home, and there's no danger. One bad guy is captured and Conrad's holed up at your place."

"How do we know there's only one?" Lorne asked.

"I'm going." Olvina started down the steep bank to the docks. First Lorne followed, then Phoebe. Wapinkino came next.

He stopped at an empty spot beside Kathleen. Kathleen looked at Wapinkino and smiled. Wapinkino smiled back.

Bradan said, "We are attempting to recover Nigel's weapon. The gun is in deep water way out by that last point."

"I can help with that, Mr. Turehue," Lorne said. "I've taken diving lessons in Lakeview."

"Get in the boat," Bradan said.

Morley guided the police boat. Valiant lay at his feet.

Olvina remained on the dock with the boys. She heaved herself onto the roof of one of the storage sheds. Phoebe followed.

Olvina noticed Bradan signaled to Morley and the young policeman brought the police boat to a stop.

Olvina said to those watching with her from the dock, "This is the spot where Uncle Nigel's gun disappeared under the surface of the water."

"Go ahead," Bradan said.

Lorne sat on the edge of the boat then, fully dressed, flipped over backwards into the water. Two minutes, later he came up for air.

Olvina smiled at Trevor, who sat at her feet.

"I wonder if he found the gun?" Trevor said.

Bradan must have asked Lorne the same question because Olvina saw him shake his head.

After a brief rest, Lorne dove again, only to return to the surface empty-handed.

He clung to the pointed bow for a rest.

"There's a little dip there," Wapinkino said, "and the water's deep."

Lorne dove again and surfaced almost immediately. He handed Bradan the gun. Olvina smiled at Phoebe, and Wapinkino and Trevor.

Morley helped Lorne into the boat. The journey back to shore began.

***

The next morning, when Olvina and Phoebe returned to work at eight o'clock, it seemed another typical day in the James Bay Frontier. By ten o'clock, the early morning coolness had turned to humid heat and the moisture on the foliage vanished into mist.

Olvina plunked herself down in the shade of some branches of a tall spruce tree. Wapinkino joined them.

"Hi, guys," he said. "I sure would love to get back to the comforts of my own home."

"We think we are bad off?" Phoebe said. "Think about those three." She looked at the policemen.

"None of them have slept for two nights," Olvina said.

Olvina heard a noise. Her, Phoebe's and Wapinkino's attention riveted on the Olson house. So did the police officers'.

The door had opened a crack.

Olvina pushed herself to her feet. The other two did the same.

Bradan took the loud speaker Kirk held towards him and lifted the horn to his lips.

"Stop right there, whoever you are!"

"It's me, Mr. Turehue," a teenaged voice answered. This caught Olvina's attention.

"Aires?"

"Yes," Wapinkino's younger brother answered. "It's me and Mom."

A voice carried through the air to the waiting group. "And me, Mr. Olson."

Bradan signaled for the SWAT team to stand ready just in case Conrad had a trick up his sleeve. Maybe even Mr. Olson was in on it.

The team stood with rifle barrels pointed towards the rickety front door.

"Come on out," Bradan told the boy and Mrs. Olson. Thirteen-year-old Aires, Mrs. Olson, Mr. Olson, and their captor, stepped out onto the rock that was all around the house.

Olvina and Phoebe hurried forward to escort the boy and his parents to safety.

Bradan, Kirk and Lyle were also on the spot.

"Lie on your stomach on the ground," Bradan commanded Conrad the instant he set foot outside.

Olvina kicked the rifle out of Conrad's hand and beyond the criminal's reach.

Phoebe grabbed the rifle and dashed back to Bradan's side. Bradan took the weapon and checked it out.

"It's not loaded," Phoebe said.

Phoebe didn't move from the spot.

Kirk quickly handcuffed Conrad before the man's mood could

change and he could get the upper hand.

Bradan turned to the leader of the SWAT team, "You guys are dismissed."

Kirk and Lyle led Conrad to the cruiser to be whisked away to jail. On their way, they passed close by where Morley and Bradan waited.

Olivina's heart thumped when Conrad paused. She glanced at her sister and saw the horrified look on her face. Both crossed their fingers, praying Conrad didn't have it in mind to tongue-lash Bradan for arresting him.

Bradan studied the man.

"I do believe this is the humblest I've ever seen you, Conrad."

Conrad turned his head and looked at Bradan, then Morley and, at last, Olvina and Phoebe.

It took Olvina and Phoebe by surprise when he asked,

"Would you and Ken, The Gospel Singing Cops, consider a performance at the prison I'll be in?" His eyes begged a positive answer.

Bradan's eyebrows shot up in surprise. He said calmly, "I'm certain we can work something in."

"Perhaps I'll hear Pastor Asquinn preaching in prison also."

Bradan nodded towards the church on the ridge. "He's both the pastor of that church and the prison chaplain."

Conrad looked in the direction Bradan indicated. He said, "I know. I used to live in Forest Lake."

The look on Conrad's face grew wistful and twisted, distorted by bitter distant memories. "Nigel and I lived the first part of our lives in Forest Lake, then when I started high school, we moved into a house in Lakeview. Nigel and I were alone. Mom or Dad didn't raise us. We raised each other."

Conrad's voice lowered. Olvina and Phoebe had to strain their ears to hear what he said.

"I'm sick and tired of my life. I want something different. Like Nigel and Sihon."

"Talk to Pastor Asquinn," Bradan said, "or my brother-in-law, Tim. He's associate pastor."

"Either one would be nice."

Bradan nodded and Conrad was escorted to the cruiser.

TV cameras, newspaper and radio reporters followed the trio as they made their way to the car. Journalists with their cameras kept pace to get pictures.

One lady reporter spoke to Olvina. Olvina rushed to Bradan, Phoebe not far behind.

"The TV news is waiting to interview the police," Olvina said, nearly out of breath.

***

Dinner was cooking at Olvina's house. The quintuplets and Audrey swirled around the kitchen preparing when the phone rang.

Martin rushed to pick up the receiver. He spoke into it and listened, then said, "Sure thing. Right away. And you will have supper with us."

Soon after that he hung up and said loudly so Audrey could hear him, "Set another place, dear, company's coming for dinner."

"Who was that, Dad?" Olvina heard Sihon ask from the kitchen.

"We will all find out in a moment," Martin replied.

Shortly after, a car drew up outside. Doors opened and closed, then the car backed out onto the road and drove away. A knock sounded at the back door.

"I'll get it," Eunice shouted.

She opened the inside back door to reveal who was there. Nigel stepped into the kitchen.

"Dad!" Sihon said, delighted.

"Uncle Nigel," Crystal squealed.

Sihon and Crystal ran to greet the man who had just joined them. Nigel knelt and embraced them both.

"It's good to see you. I'm so glad the two of you are safe."

"We are sitting down for supper. Join us," Olvina said.

"I'd be glad to," Nigel said.

"You sit right here between Crystal and Sihon," Audrey said.

***

Later that evening, when family Bible study was over, everyone that held family bible study which were all that went to the little church in Forest Lake—lingered just a little bit longer.

At Turehue's Bradan said the final prayer. "Tonight we're going to take time to thank you, God, that nobody was hurt during that hostage taking and that Sihon and Crystal's safe again. Amen."

Bradan finished the prayer along with "Amens" from Gerald and Lyle.

Children scampered outside to play and enjoy the short time before bedtime.

Before the girls disappeared outside, Martha said, "Joanne it is your turn this evening to help clean up."

"But, Mom," Joanne protested, "when is it Shannon's turn to clean up? She's always off somewhere and never does work around the house."

"Go on," Bradan said. "All of you have the rest of the evening free."

"You deserve some relaxatation time," Martha said. "Leave the dishes."

***

Olson's had just finished family Bible study, which Wapinkino led because his father wasn't staying with the family. So, for the time being, Wapinkino sat in an easy chair with Susan and Eileen perched on his knee as he prayed and read scriptures.

When the quintuplets arrived, Mrs. Olson switched on the radio to listen to the news. Olvina sat on the couch beside Wapinkino. The youth didn't mind but the knowing smiles that passed between Olvina, Phoebe, and Cassia said each one knew he wished Kathleen sat there instead of Olvina.

"Listen," Mrs. Olson said.

Everyone stopped talking and listened. Mrs. Olson turned up the volume.

"This CLEP radio, and I'm Randy Jamison. This is a taped interview from this afternoon when Conrad Cameron surrendered," The reporter said. 'With me I have Chief Inspector Bradan Turehue, OPP. Mr. Thurehue, tell us what happened, please."

Bradan spoke reassuringly to a vast area covered by the radio station.

"We reached a peaceful settlement," He finished. "Yes, shots were fired by the hostage taken, but we have only God to thank that no one was hurt. Chief Superintendent Asquinn is on holidays, but I, Chief Inspector Turehue, want to thank the members of the Forest Lake Ontario Provincial Police for giving more than one hundred percent co-operation. More like one thousand percent. Superintendent Asquinn's favorite word for that is 'stellar.' "

Bradan stopped talking, then spoke to Olvina, "Morley Barkley and I had very capable help. Along with four brand new police officers were six dedicated cadets. One Olvina Asquinn is here with me. I'll let her say a few words."

"But Uncle Bradan," Olvina said. "Me? Speak in front of the mike? On the air? For the police?"

"Sure," Bradan said. "Go on now. You will do fine."

There was a pause and a noise of shuffling about. At Olson's Olvina listened as Phoebe bravely started speaking. "Thank you, Uncle Bradan, for giving up the mic to me. We, the citizens of Forest Lake, think highly of our Ontario Provincial Police and are proud to be under their care. We can return to our homes now reassured that an escaped criminal is in custody and that Forest Lake is a protected place to raise our children. We salute the police."

The newscast ended, Mrs. Olson rose from her chair and walked over to the radio. She turned it off. The radio wentsilent and she went back to her chair.

Wapinkino moved over to the tape deck, picked out a tape, and snapped in into the player. Soon, The Gospel Singing Cops playing and singing gospel music softly filled the room.

"Uncle Tim and Tadcu, Pastor Asquinn, are going to visit the prison in Lakeview a month from this Sunday," Olvina told Wapinkino. "Want to come along?"

Chapter Eleven

"Tadcu invited The Gospel Singing Cops to accompany him and even sing some hymns," Eunice said.

"So I'll be there along with Mr. Turehue and Morley. Mr. Turehue asked me to sing along with him. Morley, too. Mr. Turehue has even mentioned inviting Gerald and Lyle, along with Murray and Kirk, to join The Gospel Singing Cops."

"And Uncle Vincent. They will add a lot to the group," Phoebe said.

"The group's numbers are really swelling," Cassia said. "They all have a strong singing voice."

"How did you, a fifteen-year-old civilian, get involved with these singing cops? I mean, those two are seasoned veteran officers, and the glistening brass of the Forest Lake OPP, I might add. And how did they get the name 'The Gospel Singing Cops'?" Mrs. Olson asked.

"Don't you like the idea of your son singing with cops, Mom?"

"I do. I'm intrigued."

"You wouldn't know much about what goes on in church," Wapinkino said.

"Why attend church?" Mrs. Olson demanded. "There is no God. If so, why did He allow this family to fall into such a mess?"

"Anyway," Wapinkino continued, "they were dubbed The Gospel

Singing Cops by their enemies that hated them. At first their enemies meant the name to degrade them and make them look foolish and mock them, but Mr. Turehue, true to his fashion, turned it around and suggested to Mr. Asquinn they should use the tag as a name to sing under."

Wapinkino sighed and said, "Mr. Turehue teaches me guitar lessons. I'm dreaming of him inviting me to sing with The Gospel Singing Cops."

Olvina said, "Uncle Bradan talks about changing the name to 'The Turehue Singers.'"

There was a pause. Mrs. Olson fidgeted in her chair.

"I don't consider myself a religious woman."

Olvina changed the subject. She was grateful for Wapinkino, who made sure all his younger brothers and sisters attended church and Sunday school. "Did Mr. Olson go back to the resort for the rest of the summer, Mrs. Olson?"

"Yes. He talked about taking the family with him."

"Yes, again. He never does," Wapinkino said bitterly. He stood. "I'm going over to your place, girls. I'm going to ask Kathleen for a date. Let's hurry before it is time for us all to be inside."

The four, almost side by side, dashed along the dirt trail to the quint's house, crossed the railroad tracks and sprinted along the road before turning into the driveway at Martin's. Olvina was a wee bit ahead when they arrived at the back door as it opened.

Wapinkino's eyes shone with anticipation when he saw Kathleen, then he stopped in his tracks when Kathleen stepped outside, then Earl, and proceeded along the driveway beside the house.

"Too late," Olvina said. "Earl got there ahead of you."

Earl and Kathleen must have heard them talking because they stopped and turned towards the sound. Earl raised his hand and waved. With the other hand he grabbed Kathleen's arm and guided her somewhat roughly down the driveway to the road, but not before Olvina noticed her look towards Wapinkino, a yearning expression on her face.

Wapinkino turned and started towards home. Olvina, Phoebe and Cassia exchanged looks, and then followed.

They were back in Olson's living room when the doorbell pealed. Olvina was the closest to the door, so she sprang to her feet and went to admit the visitor. She swung open the door.

"Uncle Bradan," Olvina said.

Mrs. Olson had followed closely behind. "Come on in, Bradan."

Bradan stepped inside.

"What can I do for you?" she asked.

"I want to see your husband's gun collection."

Without even thinking she should go back to the living room, Olvina followed along as quietly as she could while Uncle Bradan was taken to see the gun cabinet, a cubby hole beneath the stairs leading to the second level. Last, he examined the drawer where the bullets were stored.

As he stood, he said, "Entrance forced and the glass front of the storage cabinet broken, just like Wapinkino said. He's telling the truth." He looked at Mrs. Olson. "May we talk?"

"Follow me to the front room and we'll sit and be comfortable," Mrs. Olson said.

Olvina sat in her old seat. None of the teens felt they should leave the room while Mrs. Olson and the policeman talked. Neither grownup gave any indication they should leave the room.

"First, I want to know how your husband got together with Conrad and Nigel," Bradan said. "Start from the beginning."

"Certainly. I'd be glad to tell you what I know. My husband drove from Sault Ste Marie. He parks his truck at a friend's place and rides the Algoma Central train into the wilderness area to the lodge he works for in the summer. Once, while waiting for a train to clear the crossing west of Forest Lake, the passenger door suddenly opened and Conrad popped into the cab beside him."

The teens sat quietly. Olvina was content to have Bradan do the questioning.

"What was he wearing?" Bradan said.

"Plain civilian clothes," Mrs. Olson said.

"Not prison garb or anything like that?"

Mrs. Olson shook her head. "I'm not sure if he was on the train and jumped off, then saw my husband stopped and decided to take the opportunity for a ride, but that's how I feel it happened. Anyway, they were both headed for Forest Lake, so Lawrence gave him a lift."

"Conrad was alone?" Bradan asked.

"Yes. That was the day of the Dominion Day celebrations. "

"That's when Uncle Nigel talked to us, while we looked after Morley's horse," Olvina said.

Mrs. Olson continued, "He thought he knew all that was taking place at the ceremonies and a little about our family. Lawrence met this fellow who was inside this house the day of the ceremonies. Lawrence doesn't know him well. He talked a lot about being in jail but got out for some stupid reason. He also boasted about how he and his drug trafficking was raking in millions of dollars at these festivities. Everyone for miles around were at this celebration, a huge crowd."

"The kind of crowds people like that like to target," Bradan said. "We arrested six men that day for dealing drugs."

"You're saying these six men are merely small cogs in a big wheel?"

"Yes. The fellows taken into custody are really the big fish. When we arrested them that was rather a significant accomplishment." Bradan took a picture from his uniform shirt and handed it to Mrs. Olson. "Is this the other man?"

"It sure is. He's exactly as my husband described him. Who is he, anyway? Lawrence says he's unstable. Crazy. Let me think. I've seen his picture in the paper a lot. Doesn't he have something to do with gambling and casinos?"

"He sure does. He's Conrad Cameron."

A question had nagged at the back of Olvina's mind during the interview. She couldn't hold it back any longer. "Where has he been all these months, Mrs. Olson? Why come back to Forest Lake now?"

"Mr. Olson wandered all over northern and northwest Ontario. For the past month, during the summer, he worked guiding tourists in a summer camp in northwestern Ontario. The money was good, but the work only seasonal."

"Why isn't he working this summer?"

"He is, but asked for a couple of weeks off. He missed the family so much he couldn't stay away any longer."

Wapinkino let out a loud quaff at this. Others glanced his way.

Mrs. Olson said humbly, "I truly believed it was God that brought him here at this particular time to be with my family when they needed me and he would stay. Now I feel bitter towards Him and feel He's let me down."

Olvina exchanged looks with her sister. She could read by the expression on her face she thought the same thing. Was it really God that brought Mr. Olson at that particular time to be with his family when they needed him? He didn't sound sincere about loving his family. Mr. Olson's son seemed to hold the same view.

Wapinkino stirred, coming out of the daze he'd been in since leaving Martin's yard. Seeing Earl dragging Kathleen off on a date when he'd went to Martin's place to ask her out must have really hurt him.

"But he's gone again," Wapinkino said.

After a pause, Mrs. Olson continued. "When will Ken be back from holidays?"

"Not for a while. He'd just started his holidays when Conrad demanded he come back. He will be back in time for our first prison concert appearance."

Uncle Bradan stood and prepared to leave.

***

Three weeks after Conrad gave himself up, Pastor Asquinn talked behind the pulpit. "We will now bring this morning church service to a close. There won't be a service here this evening. We will be conducting our Wednesday evening service at the prison. We have transportation for lots of people. If you want to attend, sign the form at the back. We are glad to have Ken and his family back from holidays. The Gospel Singing Cops will sing and play for us Wednesday evening."

Bradan stood, turned to face the congregation, and spoke. "I invite Morley Barkley, and a civilian, Wapinkino Olson, to join us in singing Wednesday evening. If interested, speak to me at the back of the church immediately."

Bradan started down the aisle towards the back of the church. Morley started after him. Wapinkino followed.

***

Three days later, the audience—Olvina along with the inmates in the prison Conrad occupied—listened to the preaching and singing. The room was heavily rimmed with guards.

Only a few feet from Olvina, Pastor Asquinn said, "Thank you all for being here and listening. We will now listen to The Gospel Singing

Cops. The founding member is Chief Inspector Bradan Turehue. His singing partner is Chief Superintendent Asquinn."

Bradan led the way to where the instruments waited. Pastor Asquinn introduced them.

Olvina watched the singers take their place on stage.

Bradan started talking. "I am happy to say my singing partner is here tonight. He's been away for a few weeks now, vacationing. I've invited two others to join us—Morley Barclay, and a civilian teen, Wapinkino Olson."

That said, the musicians started playing their instruments. Soon, Ken and Bradan were singing a hymn. Morley and Wapinkino accompanied them on their guitars.

Olvina sat with her family.

***

Martha sat in the row in front of her twin brother, Martin.

Martha looked around. She noticed few of the prisoners listened eagerly. She looked over at Martin and they rolled their eyes at the scene of inmates slumped in their seats. The inmates' eyes were closed. Martha wondered if they were snoozing or dreaming of better living conditions. Maybe they were wishing to be anywhere but listening to the gospel being preached.

Martha noticed Conrad sat up straight in his chair, listening to the words.

Come to think of it, Martha thought, she hadn't seen Conrad face-to-face since his arrest. Pastor Asquinn was always there alone to comfort him and give him guidance in obtaining salvation God's way. Martha's heart sang knowing Conrad had received Jesus as his personal savior and fully believed the way to Heaven is through the shed blood of Jesus on the cross. Since Conrad's conversion, Martha noticed a dramatic change in him. His dark looks vanished and his face shined with the glory of God.Martha watched this once dark man carefully. She had studied the man all the way through the one-hour service and now the singing. She was convinced this was the humblest she had seen Uncle Conrad in his life.Martha did not see Nigel anywhere. She was happy to have it that way. In the old days, the two would have acted more like high priest and slave. Martha knew Nigel would have sat in a row behind his half-brother. Nigel was not in prison here. He had not arrived in Forest Lake to harm anyone. Like he told the police, he'd come to make sure his son and niece were all right. Martha had been filled with gladness when Nigel's talk with Bradan had worked in Nigel's favor. Nigel showed a lot of remorse for being teamed with Conrad in his younger years. For this he remained free.

When the singing ended and the guards had vacated the room, only Conrad remained.

Martha and her twin watched as two guards stomped to where he sat. "Come with us. It's time you were back at your cell."

Chapter Twelve

Conrad was about to rise to his feet, but Ken's words stopped him. "Stay right where you are, Conrad." He'd set his guitar in its case and left the stage and joined the guards and prisoner.

Ken said to the guards, "Leave him where he is."

"Yes, sir," both guards quickly agreed.

From where they were had moved to and were waiting as the musical instruments were being put in their cases and taken out to the van, Martin and Martha noticed Ken studying Conrad and guessed what he had in mind.

At that moment, Bradan's words broke through their thoughts. "Olvina, Cassia, let's hurry and load all this equipment in the van."

"Sure thing," the quintuplets answered as one.

"We will have it loaded in no time and we can start home," Martin said, presuming this was what they would do.

Cassia picked up Ken's guitar and started towards the entrance and the van while Olvina took down the microphones.

Martin and Martha noticed Conrad had not moved. He sat motionless and only stirred when Ken sat down beside him. "I can tell you want to talk."

"How long do we have to talk?"

"You are in my territory now. We can talk as long as I care to."

Conrad spoke with a break in his voice. "I don't know what got into me and made me believe I could get to see my daughter the way I tried. You're right, Ken. You told me when we were boys that my lifestyle wouldn't get me anywhere. I laughed at you."

"I can see it hasn't," Ken said.

"I know. I'm nothing but a low scum drug dealer—and user, I might add. My life is in shambles. I have nothing, not even a family, anymore. My wife has divorced me, my nephew bears another's last name, and my little girl is being raised as someone else's daughter."

Martin touched Martha's shoulder lightly at Conrad's words and they looked at each other, each feeling the deep, genuine sorrow and regret in the man's voice.

"I really am sorry about how your life has turned out, but if you continue in God's ways He can straighten out your life and restore it one thousand times sweeter than it was before."

Conrad guffawed, which made Ken, Martin and Martha smile.

"It wasn't sweet before. I didn't have a life. You and your friend Bradan, the two I sneered the most at while we were kids, are a different story. That's what I really call being successful—faithful friends and unfailing employee loyalty after what I saw for the past week, who would give up their lives for you and do it joyfully."

Ken said, and the twins knew he spoke for every officer in the department, "Yes, they would, Conrad. Every last one. At least a dozen of them have proven this."

Conrad continued. "And children that obey and respect you. The children are bubbling over with the joy of life yet that exuberance is disciplined and the ones that work for you are so happy."

Conrad looked in Bradan's direction. "And I used to make fun of you, Bradan, because as song leader in church. I see now it's an important position."

Bradan shrugged it off as if it didn't matter.

"I can see that is a responsible job," Conrad said. "I didn't think I'd ever say this, but I wish I have what you and Bradan do. What I've pursued all my life proved to be evasive as well as fickle—money, power and prestige."

"That's what we call being successful. It's all for nothing when you don't have the right man on your side," Ken said.

"And who's he?"

"He's the Anointed one. Christ Jesus is His name, the King of Glory, and undefeatable in battle."

Martin and Martha saw Conrad was visibly growing uncomfortable. He couldn't look Ken in the eye. He likely wished he hadn't initiated this conversation. He glanced around for the guards.

"He's probably wishing the two guards standing at the back would come and take him away," Martin said to Martha.

"We know this was impossible until their boss told them it was okay," she said.

Conrad said sadly, "It's strange that I've just come to know Him. Me. Of all people."

Martha jumped off the stage and joined the two men. Martin was a step behind her.

"You never know whom God has in mind to save," Martha said. "It's never too late as long as you're on this earth."

"We all prayed for you since we were children," Martin said.

Conrad lifted his eyes to Ken's face once again. "Is it true? Do you really think so? Has God saved me?"

"It sure is. I'll answer your first question. I, my dad, and everyone else at Golden Ridge Baptist Church believe you are now a saved man. God worked in you when you requested that you sit in on Dad's preaching visits to this prison, and at your request The Gospel Singing Cops sing here regularly. God quickened you, opened your heart and mind to receive what Dad told you in private talks with him. Jesus became you own personal Savior and you've yielded to God's will."

Then Martin and Martha witnessed a scene they had not heard of happening to Conrad before. His dark, evil facial features, which had seemed etched in stone, never changing, never smiling, now crumbled and tears glinted in the corners of his eyes.

"I truly consider myself privileged to be included in God's plan of salvation," Conrad said.

Martin said, "Part of the ransomed from the fall of man. You were chosen to inherit eternal life. God wouldn't have sent you to hell; you would have went there because of your own sins. But He did choose you, the elect, His sheep, to be saved. You were saved by a sovereign act of God's grace and for no other reason."

"But what about Nigel?"

"What about him?" Martha said.

They had to wait several minutes to hear Conrad's answer. He swallowed several times before he could form the words.

"I feel a great burden for him."

"Why?"

"I feel responsible for him not being saved."

"There's no need to."

"But..." Conrad started.

"Nigel was saved a long time ago when we were children."

"What? When?"

"Remember the few weeks he lived with us?"

"Yes."

"He was saved then. And it doesn't matter what kind of life you forced him back into when you enticed him home."

"He came home willingly."

"No, he didn't," Martha said.

"He went kicking and screaming, and after that I have no idea what kind of hex you put on him to get him to follow you home," Martin added. "Anyway, one thing we can be assured of in God's salvation is once saved always saved. Don't get me wrong, this doesn't mean you can live any way you choose."

"Isn't that the idea your brother and his friend had when they were in high school? I seem to remember Ken or Bradan weren't living the way Christians should."

Martha looked anxiously at her oldest brother. Martin looked anxiously at Ken. How was this knowledge to affect Conrad's future walk with God, and the people of Forest Lake, especially the Asquinn family?

"So true," Martha said. "But my brother and Bradan found out they were so wrong and paid the consequences."

Conrad breathed a sigh of relief. "I'm glad to hear Nigel is also saved. I can rest easier at night now."

The twins knew his words were right from the heart.

Martin and Martha waited, expecting more questions.

Martin glanced towards the stage. Bradan waited with the five sisters, Wapinkino, Trevor and Lorne, and another classmate, Owen Winschell. The twins waited for Conrad to say something then looked at him.

No words came.

"Is there anything else?" Martha said.

Conrad said shyly, "Yes. Is there any way I could legally get my daughter back?"

"My brother and his wife legally adopted Crystal."

Martha felt sorry for the man when Conrad's face fell in keen disappointment.

"You have every right to Crystal if you can prove you are a worthy parent, but you do have a long prison term. Crystal could be married by the time you are out," Martin said.

Conrad looked glum.

"What will I do with my life? It's ruined. I have nothing to look forward to but gloom."

"Don't look at it like that," Martha said.

"Look upon your stay in prison as a God-given opportunity," Martin said.

"How can I do that?"

"You've become a Christian. Share your experience, tell the other inmates about Jesus and salvation," Martha said.

Conrad's face brightened. "What a good idea. I'll do that."

Martin reached for the briefcase he'd set on the chair next to him. Before he could reach it and pull the case towards him, Olvina picked up the leather case and handed it to him. With loud snaps of the locks he opened the lid and looked inside. "I have material here that would help you get a Bible study started." He took some papers, small paperback books and hardcover books from the case, and handed them to his onetime enemy.

Martin exchanged smiles with his sister, thinking Conrad started to look happier with each passing moment.

"Thanks, Martin. I'll start a Bible study. You can count on me."

Conrad paused and his forehead creased in thought. He turned his gaze to Ken. "I could get out in a few years if I behave myself. Right?"

Ken's answer made Martha feel sorry for the other man. "Maybe. I will help you all you can. It's out of my hands now and in the hands of the courts. Do you have any place to live when you do get out?"

"I still have the farm."

The twins didn't have to look at each other to smile.

"The very place Sihon loved," Martha said.

"How nice the farm was never sold," Martin added.

"The buildings have been standing empty for a long time," Conrad said.

"That's a start," Martha said. "Let's take this one step at a time."

"You know that Nigel has chosen to remain in Forest Lake?" Martin asked.

Conrad nodded.

"He has a job working with the railroad maintenance crew for now."

"How does he like it?"

"I'm confident he likes it well enough to remain with it and make something of his life," Martin said.

"A good idea," Conrad said.

Ken glanced at his watch. "I must get going." He stood and Conrad did the same. The guards standing by the door immediately stood straighter. Conrad followed the other out of the room where they passed by those on the stage.

Martin and Martha watched as the guards ushered Conrad through another door and the door closed slowly behind the three. Martha's heart felt joy, along with her twin brother, for the man as Conrad faded from view, walking along between the guards, but before he was out of sight, Conrad looked back and the two pairs of eyes met. The twins noticed their older brother smiled encouragement at the other man.

Bradan and Wapikino joined them. "We're ready to roll," Martin said.

"Could we stop somewhere along the way for something to eat? I'm starved," Wapinkino said.

"We can do that," Bradan said.

"What do you think of the idea, Olvina? Cassia, Phoebe, Kathleen, Eunice?" Martin asked.

"Sounds good to me," the girls said in unison.

Martin stood to one side of the street door, Martha on the other. Martin waved a hand. "Lead on, young ladies."

Olvina and her sisters giggled as they sprinted to the van full of Forest Lake church members that had attended the prison service. Lorne had attended along with Trevor, Daniel and Mr. and Mrs. Olverton. There was friendly wrestling amongst the boys.

"It's so good to see them acting like teenagers again," Martha said.

TO BE CONTINUED.........what are the girls, and their children, to expect from the future with their backslidden husbands? Who is the mysterious person that's watched Ken and Braden from boyhood and what happens to him?

Find out whether the ending will make you weep or cheer or both, by reading Book Three, The Asquinn Twins: No Greener pastures.

Other Books By Grace Brooks
The Asquinn Twins Series

The Asquinn twins Come to Forest Lake. Book One
Where The Trail Forks: Book Two
No greener Pastures: Book Three.
Sihon. Book Four.

Books Five Six and Seven are works in progress.

A Dog For Keeps under the pen name Lynette Tamar Mark (audio book) Snow Queen's Forever Home: Iinda Grace Brooks

www.ingramcontent.com/pod-product-compliance
Lightning Source LLC
Chambersburg PA
CBHW071531080526
44588CB00011B/1642